E Alberton Harrison

The Armorial and Genealogical Roll of the High Sheriffs for the Counties in England and Wales, 1882-3

Including those sheriffs of cities, towns, and counties thereof who bear

coat armour, 1881-2, 1882-3

E Alberton Harrison

The Armorial and Genealogical Roll of the High Sheriffs for the Counties in England and Wales, 1882-3
Including those sheriffs of cities, towns, and counties thereof who bear coat armour, 1881-2, 1882-3

ISBN/EAN: 9783337329372

Printed in Europe, USA, Canada, Australia, Japan

Cover: Foto ©Suzi / pixelio.de

More available books at **www.hansebooks.com**

The Armorial and Genealogical

Roll of the High Sheriffs

FOR THE

Counties in England and Wales,

1882-3.

INCLUDING THOSE SHERIFFS OF CITIES, TOWNS, AND COUNTIES THEREOF
WHO BEAR COAT ARMOUR, 1881-2, 1882-3.

Illustrated with the Coats of Arms of the Subscribers.

COMPILED BY

E. ALBERTON HARRISON,

Heraldic Artist to the Order of St. John of Jerusalem in England.

LONDON:

PUBLISHED BY E. A. HARRISON AND CO.,

20 HYDE PARK PLACE, W.

1883.

Introduction.

THE office of High Sheriff is one of great antiquity and honour. The holder of the dignity was called Vice-Comes, as being the deputy of the Comes or Earl to whom the custody of the shire was committed at the first division of England into counties; but the Earls in process of time, by their high employment and attendance on the King's person, not being able to transact the business of the county, were released from the burden thereof, reserving to themselves the honour, but transferring the labour to the Sheriffs, or Vice-Comes.

These officers were formerly chosen by the inhabitants of the several counties, for it was ordained by Statute 28th Edward I. that the people should have an election of Sheriff; this election, however, was not entirely vested in the Commons, but required the Royal approbation. These elections, growing tumultuous, were discontinued by Statute 9th Edward II., which enacted that the Sheriff should henceforth be nominated by the Chancellor, Treasurer, and the Judges; and by Statute of Cambridge, 12th Richard II., these dignitaries, together with the Keeper of the Privy Seal, Clerk of the Rolls, and others, were sworn to act indifferently, and " to name no man that suith to be put into office, but such only as they shall judge to be the best and most sufficient."

Sheriffs, by virtue of several old Statutes, are to continue in office no longer than one year: and Statute 1st Richard II. ordains that no man having served the office one year can be compelled to serve again within three years after.

The powers and duties of a Sheriff were those of a Ministerial Officer of the Superior Courts of Justice, and Keeper of the King's Peace, or the King's Bailiff.

The Sovereign's Letters Patent appointing the new Sheriff used commonly to bear date the 6th of November.

THE ceremony of nominating High Sheriffs dates from the ninth year of Edward II., as regards the English counties,* and was made an annual occurrence by the 14th Edward III., Statute 1, Chap. 7. Sheriffs for the Welsh Counties were formerly nominated by the Lord President, Council, and Justices of Wales, and the names so chosen were certified to the Sovereign. These Welsh officials were abolished during the reign of William and Mary, and the Sheriffs were nominated for many years by the Justices of Great Sessions, and certified to the Privy Council. But now, by Act. 8 Vict., Chap. 11, they are nominated in the same manner and on the same day as the English Sheriffs.

The appointment, or "pricking," is usually made at the first or second Royal Council in every year, and is performed by the Sovereign passing the point of a golden bodkin through one of the names in each County appearing on a Roll prepared by the Queen's Remembrancer, thus appointing the Sheriff for the ensuing year.

---

* With the exception of the Sheriff for the County of Lancaster, who is appointed by Her Majesty, as Duchess of Lancaster; of Cornwall, by H.R.H. the Prince of Wales, as Duke of Cornwall; of Middlesex, by the Corporation of the City of London.

INDEX.

Subscribers' Names are marked thus [*].

————◆————

England.

vi

North Wales.

COUNTY	SHERIFF	PAGE	COUNTY	SHERIFF	PAGE
Anglesey	*Edwards, H.	47	Flintshire	{ Grenville-Williams, Sir W., Bart. }	49
Carnarvonshire	*Evans, J.	48	Merionethshire	*Williams, C. R.	50
Denbighshire	Jesse, J. F.	49	Montgomeryshire	*Fairles-Humphreys, N.	51

South Wales.

COUNTY	SHERIFF	PAGE	COUNTY	SHERIFF	PAGE
Breconshire	*Lewis, J.	52	Glamorganshire	{ Spearman, Sir J. I. E., Bart. }	55
Cardiganshire	Lloyd, C.	54	Pembrokeshire	*Philipps, C. E. G.	56
Carmarthenshire	Morris, T.	54	Radnorshire	Rogers, C. C.	58

For Sheriffs of Cities, Towns, Boroughs, and Counties thereof, see page 59.

Bedfordshire.

✦✦✦✦✦

Francis Bassett, Esq.,

of The Heath, a Magistrate for the County, and High Sheriff 1882–3. Represented Bedfordshire in the House of Commons from 1872 to 1875. Head of the Banking firm of BASSETT and Co. at Leighton Buzzard. Born 1820. Educated at Grove House, Tottenham. Married, 1842, ELLEN, second daughter of EDWARD HARRIS, Esq., of Stoke Newington, and has issue two sons and five daughters.

Third son of the late

John Dollin Bassett, Esq., of The Cedars, Leighton Buzzard (who died 1878), by his wife, MARY, daughter of THOMAS THEOBALD, Esq.

———

Lineage.

The ancient family of BASSETT, with its numerous branches, claim descent from THURSTINE DE BASSET, Grand Falconer to William the Conqueror, whose name appears on the Roll of Battle Abbey, and who is supposed to have been of Baronial rank in Normandy (as Ordericus Vitalis writes). RALPH, the son of THURSTINE, held the high office of Chief Justice of England—" a power so great that he sat in what court he thought fit for the administration of justice." Another son, Sir JOHN, was Chancellor and Vice-Comes in Glamorganshire.

Arms.—Barry wavy of six or and gules.

Crest.—An unicorn's head, couped argent, horned and crined or.

Motto.—Pro Rege et Populo.

Seat.—The Heath, Leighton Buzzard, Bedfordshire.

Club.—Reform.

B

Berkshire.

✺✺✺✺✺

Colonel William Gray of Farley Hill Place, J.P. and D.L. for Lancashire, and a Magistrate for Berkshire. High Sheriff 1882–3. Late Major Royal Lancashire Militia, and now Hon. Colonel of the 14th Lancashire Rifle Volunteers. Was Mayor of Bolton 1850–52, and M.P. for Bolton 1857–74. Married, 1861, MAGDALENE, daughter of the late JOHN ROBIN, Esq., of West Kirby, Co. Cheshire, and has, with other issue, JOHN ROBIN, born 1864.

Lineage.

Rev. JOHN GRAY, M.A. Born 1704. For thirty years Rector of Tanfield, Yorks. Died 1774.⊤MARY HOLMES. Died 1784.

JOHN GRAY, Esq., of Finedon, Co. Northampton. Born 1739. Died 1811.⊤ELIZABETH, daughter of JOHN GLOVER of Dublin. She died 1829.

WILLIAM GRAY, Esq., Merchant, of Wheatfield, Co. Lancaster. Born 1774. Died 1842.⊤FRANCES, daughter of DORNING RASBOTHAM, Esq., of Birch House, Co. Lancaster. She died 1838.

Col. WILLIAM GRAY (second son), present High Sheriff.

Arms.—Azure, a lion rampant within an orle of annulets argent, a bordure indented ermine, a crescent for difference.

Crest.—On a rock proper, a bear's paw erect and erased sable, grasping a snake entwined round it vert.

Motto.—Tenebo.

Seats.—Farley Hill Place, Swallowfield, Berks, and Frankby Manor, Birkenhead, Cheshire.

Clubs.—Carlton, Conservative, and Junior United Service.

Buckinghamshire.

❃❃❃❃❃❃

John Edward Bartlett, Esq., of Peverel Court, J.P. and D.L. for Buckinghamshire, and a Magistrate for the Borough of Buckingham. High Sheriff 1882-3. Born 1824. Married first, 1857, Sybilla Mackenzie, daughter of Alexander Mackenzie Kirkland, Esq. (she died 1860): secondly, 1866, Sarah Emily, only daughter of James Napier, Esq.; and has, with other issue, a son Edward Noel Napier, born 1870.

Eldest son of the late

Edward Bartlett, Esq., of Buckingham, by his wife Eliza Mary, daughter of the late S. Holloway, Esq., of the same town.

Lineage.

The immediate ancestors of this family were for many years of Brackley in Co. Northampton, from whence the grandfather of Mr. J. E. Bartlett removed to Buckingham, and established a Bank there. It would appear that this family is of common origin with the Barttelots of Stopham, an ancient family said to have come over to England with William the Conqueror, and settled at a place called La Ford in the parish of Stopham, Sussex, where, some time in the fourteenth century, John Barttelot, the son of Adam, married Joan, elder daughter and coheir of William Stopham of Stopham, which estate has remained in the family ever since.

Arms.—Sable, three falconer's sinister gloves pendant argent, tasselled or.

Crest.—A swan argent, couched, wings expanded in dorso.

Motto.—My trust is in God.

Seat.—Peverel Court, Aylesbury.

Clubs.—The Union and The Gresham.

Cambridgeshire and Huntingdonshire.

❄❄❄❄❄❄

Ebenezer Bird Foster, Esq., of Anstey Hall, Justice of the Peace and Deputy Lieutenant for the County of Cambridge. High Sheriff for Cambridgeshire and Huntingdonshire 1882-3. Senior partner of the well-known Banking firm at Cambridge. Born 1838. Educated at Totteridge, Herts. Married, 1870, MARY CAMPBELL, daughter of the Rev. Prebendary RICHARD SNOWDON SMITH.

Eldest son of the late

George Ebenezer Foster, Esq., of Brooklands, Co. of Cambridge, High Sheriff in 1868 (died 1870), whose father, EBENZER FOSTER, Esq., was also High Sheriff in the year 1849.

Arms.—Azure, on a pile, between two bugles in base stringed or, a bugle stringed of the field.

Crest.—On a wreath of the colours a demi-stag or, semé of pheons, and holding between the legs a bugle azure.

Motto.—Virtutis præmium honor.

Seat.—Anstey Hall, Trumpington, Cambridgeshire.

Clubs.—The Union and The City.

Cheshire.

✪✪✪✪✪

Egerton Leigh, Esq., of the West Hall, High Leigh, J.P. and D.L. High Sheriff 1882–3. Late a Captain 1st Royal Dragoons, A.D.C. Joint Lord of the Manor of High Leigh, and Patron of two Livings. Born 1843. Married, 5 August 1874, Lady Elizabeth Mary Gore White, eldest daughter of the Earl of Bantry, who died 1880, by whom he has issue.

Arms.—Or, a lion rampant gules; quartering Yates, Doughty, Jodrell, and Wright.

Crests.—1. A cubit arm, vested paly of five pieces or and sable, cuffed argent, hand proper, grasping the upper and lower fragments of a broken tilting-spear, point downwards. 2. A demi-lion rampant or, holding a pennon displayed azure, charged with two bars or, inscribed with the motto and with a shield of the arms of Leigh, on which are three escutcheons, representing the arms of the three husbands of Agnes de Leigh.

Motto.—Force abec bertu.

Seats.—West Hall, High Leigh, and Jodrell Hall, Co. Chester.

Club.—Junior United Service.

For Pedigree, see next page.

Pedigree.

The ancient family of Leigh of High Leigh descends from Thomas, the son of Richard de Lymm, first husband to Agnes, sole daughter and heir of Richard de Leigh of High Leigh. This Thomas assumed the name of Leigh, and obtained the estate of West Hall, which has remained in the family until the present time. Thirteenth in descent from Thomas Leigh was—

Rev. Peter Leigh, M.A., Vicar of Great Budworth, Rector of Lymme and of Whitchurch, Salop. ⊤ Elizabeth, daughter of the Hon. Thomas Egerton of Tatton Park, third son of John, second Earl of Bridgewater, and descended through Mary, Queen-Dowager of France, from Henry VIII.

Rev. Egerton Leigh, LL.D., of the West Hall, Rector of Lymme and Middle, Canon Residentiary and Master of the Hospital of St. Katherine at Ledbury. Baptized 30 March 1702. ⊤ Ann (first wife), daughter and coheir of Hamlet Yates, Esq., of Crowley.

Rev. Peter Leigh, LL.B., Rector of Lymme and of Middle. Died v.p. 1758. ⊤ Mary, daughter and coheir of Henry Doughty, Esq., of Broadwell, Gloucestershire.

Egerton Leigh of the West Hall and of Twemlow. Born 1752. Married 1778. Died ? ⊤ Elizabeth, daughter and coheir of Francis Jodrell, Esq., of Yeardsley and of Twemlow.

Egerton Leigh of the West Hall and of Jodrell Hall, J.P. and D.L., High Sheriff 1836, formerly Captain 3rd Dragoon Guards. Born 1779. Married 1809. ⊤ Wilhelmina Sarah, daughter of George Stratton, Esq., of Tew Park, Oxford.

Egerton Leigh of the West Hall and of Jodrell Hall, Co. Chester, Broadwell House, Co. Gloucester, and Bulcote Lodge, Co. Notts, J.P. and D.L., a Captain 2nd Dragoon Guards, and afterwards Major and Brevet-Colonel 1st Cheshire Militia, High Sheriff 1872, M.P. for Mid-Cheshire 1873 to 1876. Born 1815. Married 1842. Died 1876. ⊤ Lydia Rachel, daughter and coheir of John Smith Wright. Esq., of Bulcote Lodge, Notts.

Egerton Leigh, Esq., High Sheriff 1882-3.

Cornwall.

✦✦✦✦✦✦

Walter Deeble Boger, Esq., of Wolsdon, a Magistrate for Cornwall. High Sheriff 1882–3. Born 1832. Educated at Winchester and Trinity Coll., Cambridge (B.A. 1854, M.A. 1857). Married, 1863, AMELIA HARRIET, youngest daughter of the late THOMAS HOLMES BOSWORTH, Esq., of Westerham, Kent.

Arms.—1 and 4. Azure, three scope-staves, or dibbles, argent, for DIBBLE. 2 and 3. Sable, a cross argent, two roses in chief of the same, for WOLSDON.

Crest.—An arm, holding in the hand a dibble and a rose.

Motto.—Deus providebit, mi fili.

Seat.—Wolsdon, Antony, Devonport. (This is one of the oldest properties in Cornwall. Alwod of Wolsdon possessed it in 1087.)

Residence.—56 Upper Berkeley Street, W.

Club.—United University.

Pedigree of the Family of Boger.

CHRISTOPHER BOGER, a landowner of Plymstock,⊤ISABEL .... Will Devonshire. Died about 1560. │ proved 1563.

SYLVESTER BOGER.⊤

EDMOND BOGER.⊤

RICHARD BOGER.⊤
A

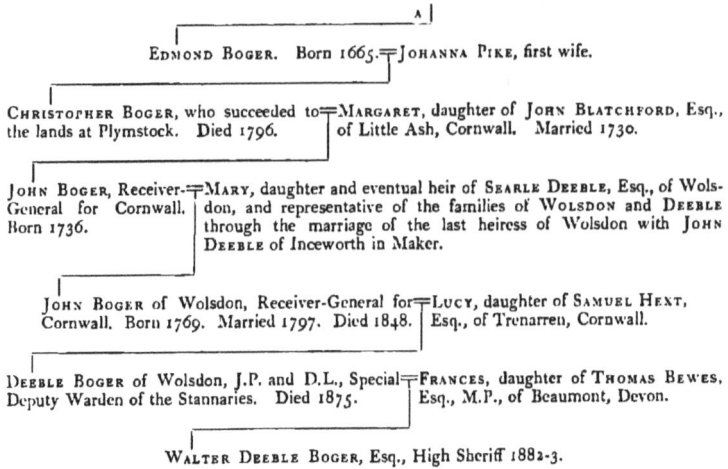

```
                                        A |
        |
    EDMOND BOGER.  Born 1665.⊤JOHANNA PIKE, first wife.
    |
CHRISTOPHER BOGER, who succeeded to⊤MARGARET, daughter of JOHN BLATCHFORD, Esq.,
the lands at Plymstock.  Died 1796.  | of Little Ash, Cornwall.  Married 1730.

    |
JOHN BOGER, Receiver-⊤MARY, daughter and eventual heir of SEARLE DEEBLE, Esq., of Wols-
General for Cornwall. | don, and representative of the families of WOLSDON and DEEBLE
Born 1736.           | through the marriage of the last heiress of Wolsdon with JOHN
                     | DEEBLE of Inceworth in Maker.

    |
    JOHN BOGER of Wolsdon, Receiver-General for⊤LUCY, daughter of SAMUEL HEXT,
    Cornwall.  Born 1769.  Married 1797.  Died 1848. | Esq., of Trenarren, Cornwall.

    |
DEEBLE BOGER of Wolsdon, J.P. and D.L., Special⊤FRANCES, daughter of THOMAS BEWES,
Deputy Warden of the Stannaries.  Died 1875.   | Esq., M.P., of Beaumont, Devon.

        |
    WALTER DEEBLE BOGER, Esq., High Sheriff 1882-3.
```

Cumberland.

George Routledge, Esq., of Hardhurst and Croft House, J.P. and
D.L. for the County of Cumberland. High Sheriff 1882-3. Born 1812.
Married first, 1836, MARIA ELIZABETH, second daughter of the late EDMUND
WARNE, Esq. (she died 1855); secondly, 1858, MARY GRACE, eldest daughter
of the late Alderman BELL of Newcastle-on-Tyne, and has issue.

Youngest son of the late

Robert Routledge, Esq., of Brampton, Co. Cumberland.

Arms.—Or, a trefoil triple-slipped vert.
Crest.—A sheaf of wheat vert.
Motto.—Perseverantia.
Seat.—Stone House, Hayton, near Carlisle.
Club.—County Club, Carlisle.

Derbyshire.

✸✸✸✸✸✸

Charles Edmund Newton, Esq., of the Manor House, Mickleover, a Magistrate and Deputy Lieutenant for the County of Derby. High Sheriff 1882-3. Lord of the Manor of Mickleover. Formerly Major Derby Rifle Volunteers. Born 1831. Educated at Rugby and Trinity College, Cambridge. Succeeded his brother 1854. Married first, 1855, ANNE ROSAMOND, only daughter of JOHN CURZON, Esq., of Breedon, Co. Leicester, by whom he has, with other issue, ROBERT CURZON, born 1857; secondly, 1866, MARY HENRIETTA, only daughter of the late Captain MOORE of the 17th Regiment.

Pedigree.

JOHN NEWTON of Horseley, M.P. for Denby 12 and 17 Edward IV.⊤

THOMAS NEWTON of Horseley.⊤MARGARET WIDDISON.

ROBERT NEWTON of Chaddesden,⊤DOROTHY, daughter of VINCENT Co. Derby. Died 1592. | LOWE, Esq., of Denby.

ROBERT NEWTON, third and youngest son, of Mickle-⊤CLEERE, daughter and heir of WILLIAM over, Barrister-at-Law and Recorder of Derby. | GILBERT, Esq., of Mickleover. Married 1609. Died 1619.

A

C

EDWARD NEWTON of Mickleover. Born=JANE, daughter of JOHN BERESFORD, Esq.,
1610. Married 1625. Died 1661. | of Newton Grange, Co. Derby.

ROBERT NEWTON of Mickleover. Born 1629.=ELIZABETH, daughter of GERVAS WHITEHEAD,
Barrister-at-Law. Died 1701-2. | Esq., of Breeston, Co. Derby.

JOHN MACHIN of Seabridge, Co. Stafford.=CLEERE, eldest daughter. Married 1685.

JOHN LEAPER.=CLEER, only daughter and heir. Married 1711.

WILLIAM LEAPER, Alderman of Derby. Died 1780.=SARAH WARD.

JOHN LEAPER-NEWTON. Born 1754. Succeeded on the death of=ANNA MARIA, daughter of
his kinsman, ROBERT NEWTON, to Mickleover, and assumed by | PHILIP HUTCHINSON, Esq.,
Royal Licence, 1789, the additional name of NEWTON. A Magis- | of Risley, Co. Derby.
trate, D.L., and High Sheriff for the County.

WILLIAM LEAPER-NEWTON of Leylands, second son,=HENRIETTA, second daughter of JOHN
Barrister-at-Law and D.L. Married 1814. Died | WHITE, Esq., of The Lawn, Co. Herts.
1851.

CHARLES EDMUND NEWTON, third and only surviving son, High Sheriff 1882-3.

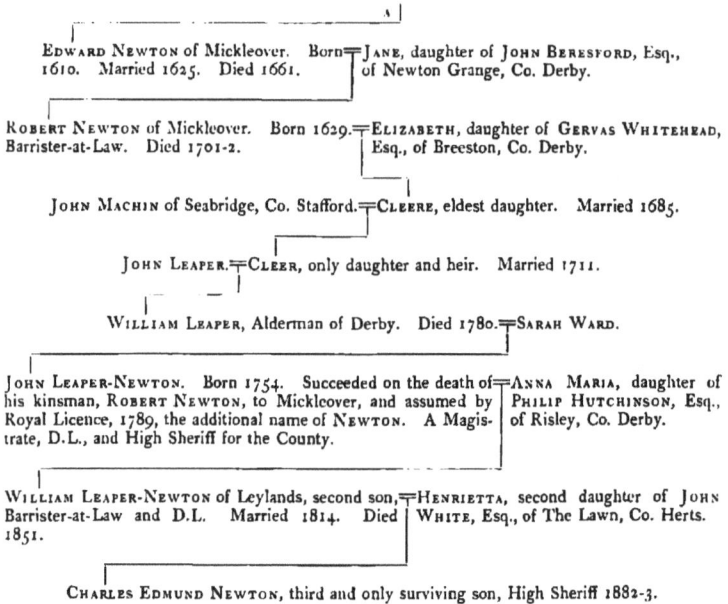

Arms.—Sable, two human shin-bones in saltier argent, the sinister surmounted of the dexter.

Crest.—A naked man, kneeling on his sinister knee, and holding a sword proper, the point downwards, hilt and pommel or.

Motto.—Hinc habeo non tibi.

Seat.—The Manor House, Mickleover.

Devonshire.

✠✠✠✠✠✠

William Halliday Halliday, Esq., of Glenthorne, Lynmouth, and West View, Torquay, J.P., D.L., and Chairman of Quarter Sessions for Devonshire. High Sheriff 1882–3. J.P. and a Magistrate for Somersetshire. Lord of the Manors and Patron of Bilsington, Kent, and of Countesbury, Devon, and Patron of Oare, Somersetshire. A Barrister-at-Law. Born 1828. Educated at Winchester and Balliol College, Oxford (B.A. 1850, M.A. 1855). Married, 1860, MARIA, daughter of Sir THOMAS HARVIE FARQUHAR, second Baronet, of Polesden, and has issue.

Pedigree.

Derived from the last Laird of Corehead, the Chief of the family of HALLIDAY, through "WALTER the Minstrel," who became Master of the Revels to Edward IV., and acquired lands in Rodburgh, Co. Gloucester.

THEOBALD HALLIDAY, went to═Miss HAY, heiress of Tullicbole, Co. Fife, only daughter
Holland, where he married. │ of Colonel HAY, in the service of the States-General.

│
JOHN HALLIDAY, educated in Holland, succeeded on his mother's═
death to the lands at Tulliebole. Was in great favour with JAMES │
VI., who is said to have knighted him. │

┌────────────────
WILLIAM HALLIDAY (second son),═. . . daughter of GABRIEL JOHNSTON,
Provost of Dundee. │ a Merchant and Burgess of Dumfries.
A │

A |

THOMAS HALLIDAY, came into England, but returned in 1697 with the army=Miss WRIGHT, an
of the Duke of Monmouth, and settled on property acquired, *jure uxoris*, heiress of the Four
at Berngan, Co. Dumfries. Towns.

SIMON HALLIDAY (second son) of Whinnyrigg, on the banks of the Frith of Solway.=GRACIE . . .

JOHN HALLIDAY of Whinnyrigg.=

SIMON HALLIDAY of Whinnyrigg, Surgeon=. . . only daughter of THOMAS
R.N., and Banker of London. HARVIE, Esq., of Jamaica.

ELIZABETH HARVIE HALLIDAY.=Sir WILLIAM RICHARD COSWAY, Knt.,
Married 1823. Died 1876. of Bilsington, Kent. Died 1834.

WILLIAM HALLIDAY COSWAY, assumed the Name and
Arms of HALLIDAY only 1872, High Sheriff 1882-3.

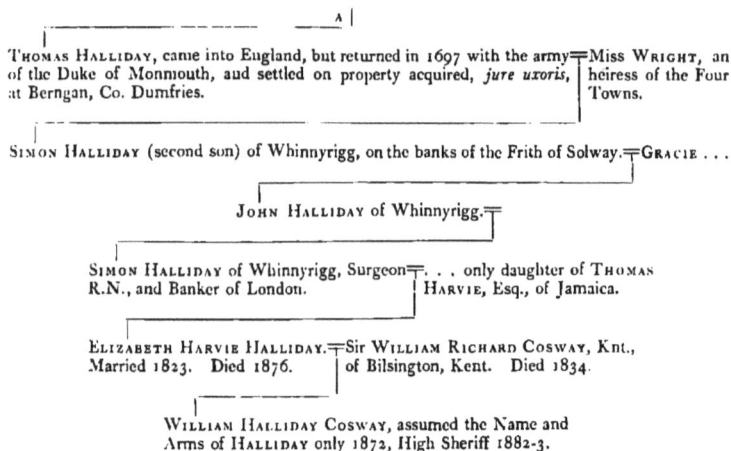

Arms.—Argent, a sword erect in pale, the pommel within a crescent in base gules, on
a canton azure a saltire of the first.

Crest.—A boar's head couped proper, langued gules, tusked or.

Motto.—Virtute parta.

Seats.—Glenthorne, Lynmouth, Barnstaple, N. Devon; West View, Torquay,
S. Devon.

Club.—Oxford and Cambridge.

Dorsetshire.

✿✿✿✿✿✿

Baron Charles Joseph Theophilus Hambro of Milton Abbey, Justice of the Peace and Deputy Lieutenant for the County. High Sheriff 1882–3. Lord of the Manors and Patron of Winterbourn, Strickland, and Milton Abbas. Lieutenant-Colonel of Dorset Yeomanry, late Captain 8th Dorset Rifle Volunteers. M.P. for Weymouth 1868–74. Born 1834. Educated at Trinity College, Cambridge. Called to the Bar at the Inner Temple, 1860. Married, 1857, Susan Amelia, youngest daughter of the late Hon. and Ven. Rev. Henry R. Yorke, Archdeacon of Huntingdon.

Eldest son of the late

Baron Charles Joachim Hambro of Milton Abbey (who died 1877), by his first wife, Caroline, daughter of M. Gostenhofer.

Arms.—Azure, a chevron or, between in chief three annulets and in base a lion passant. On an escutcheon gules, ensigned with a baron's coronet, a cross argent.

Crests.—1. On a baron's coronet a lion rampant, grasping between the paws a battle-axe. 2. A falcon with wings endorsed, resting the dexter claw upon an increscent.

Supporters.—Dexter, a savage, wreathed about the loins and temples, holding in the dexter hand a club. Sinister, a falcon with wings endorsed.

Motto.—In Deo.

Seat.—Milton Abbey, Blandford.

Clubs.—Carlton, Arthur's, Boodle's, Junior Carlton, and the Garrick.

Durham.

✠✠✠✠✠✠

Robert Anthony Burrell, Esq., of Fairthorne, Hants, and Durham, a Magistrate for the Counties of Durham and Hants. High Sheriff 1882-3. Born 1829. Educated at Repton School and Durham University.

Eldest son of the late

John Burrell, Esq., Proctor of Durham (who died in 1861), by his wife ANNE, daughter of ANTHONY TILLEY, Esq., of Durham.

Lineage.

The family of BURRELL is of very ancient date upon the borders of England and Scotland, the name occurring in records of the time of Richard II., and as early as 1250 they were settled at Berwick-on-Tweed. The name has been corrupted into BORAILLE, BORELL, and BURWELL.

Arms.—Or, a saltire gules between four leaves vert, on a chief azure a lion's head erased between two battle-axes proper.

Crest.—A lion's head erased proper.

Motto.—Diluculo surgere.

Seat.—Fairthorne, Botley, Southampton.

Essex.

✠✠✠✠✠✠

Hector John Gurdon-Rebow, Esq., of Wivenhoe Park, J.P. and D.L. for Essex. High Sheriff 1882–3. A Magistrate for Essex and Cambridgeshire, and Patron of one Living. Formerly a Sub-Lieutenant 2nd Life Guards, and late Lieutenant Essex Rifle Militia. Born 1846. Educated at Eton and Trinity College, Cambridge (B.A. 1869). Married, 1873, BLANCHE JUDITH, daughter of the Rev. PHILIP GURDON, Rector of Cranworth, Norfolk, and has, with other issue, a son MARTIN, born 1875.

Arms.—Quarterly—1 and 4. Gules, two long bows bent and interlaced or, stringed argent, between four bezants, each charged with a fleur-de-lis azure. [REBOW.] 2 and 3. Sable, three leopard's faces, jessant-de-lis or. [GURDON.]

Crests.—1. A demi-eagle displayed, issuant out of a mural crown, on the breast a bezant charged with a fleur-de-lis azure, in the beak an arrow of the second, headed and feathered argent. 2. A goat climbing up a rock, all proper.

Seat.—Wivenhoe Park, near Colchester.

Club.—Brook's.

Gloucestershire.

✠✠✠✠✠✠

Sir Thomas Hyde Crawley-Boevey, Bart., High Sheriff for the County 1882–3, and a Magistrate. One of the Verderers of the Forest of Dean. Late Ensign in the 69th Foot. Born 2nd July 1837. Succeeded his father as fifth Baronet 14th October 1862. Married, 25 July 1865, FRANCES ELIZABETH, only daughter of the Rev. THOMAS PETERS, Rector of Eastington, Gloucestershire, and has, with other issue, a son FRANCIS HYDE, born 1868.

Arms (granted 1789).—Erminois, on a fess azure between three cranes proper a saltier between two cross-crosslets fitché or, for CRAWLEY. On a chief ermine a bend gules, charged with three guttés d'or between two martlets sable ; quartering LLOYD, SAVAGE, and BARROW.

Crest.—On a mount vert a crane proper, collared, beaked, and holding in the dexter claw a saltier or.

Motto.—Esse quam videri.

Seat.—Flaxley Abbey, near Newnham, Gloucestershire.

Hampshire.

✠✠✠✠✠✠

Thomas Thistlethwayte, Esq., a Magistrate for Hants, Lord of the Manor of Southwick. High Sheriff 1882-3. Born 1809. Married, secondly, ELIZABETH CATHERINE, daughter of the late Lieutenant-General the Hon. Sir HERCULES PAKENHAM, K.C.B., and has issue.

Arms.—Or, on a bend azure three pheons of the field.
Crest.—A demi-lion azure, holding a pheon or.
Seat.—Southwick Park.

Herefordshire.

✠✠✠✠✠✠

Theophilus William Lane, Esq., of Ryelands, J.P. and D.L. for the County of Hereford. High Sheriff 1882-3. Born 1817. Educated at Trinity College, Cambridge (B.A. 1841, M.A. 1844). Married, 1848, EMILY, daughter of CHARLES BOWEN, Esq., of Kilna Court, Queen's County.

Arms.—Per pale azure and gules, three saltires couped argent; quartering RODD of Rodd—Argent, two trefoils in fesse vert, a chief or.
Crest.—Out of a crescent or two griffins' heads, the dexter gules, sinister azure.
Motto.—Celeritate.
Seat.—Ryelands, Leominster.
Club.—Conservative.

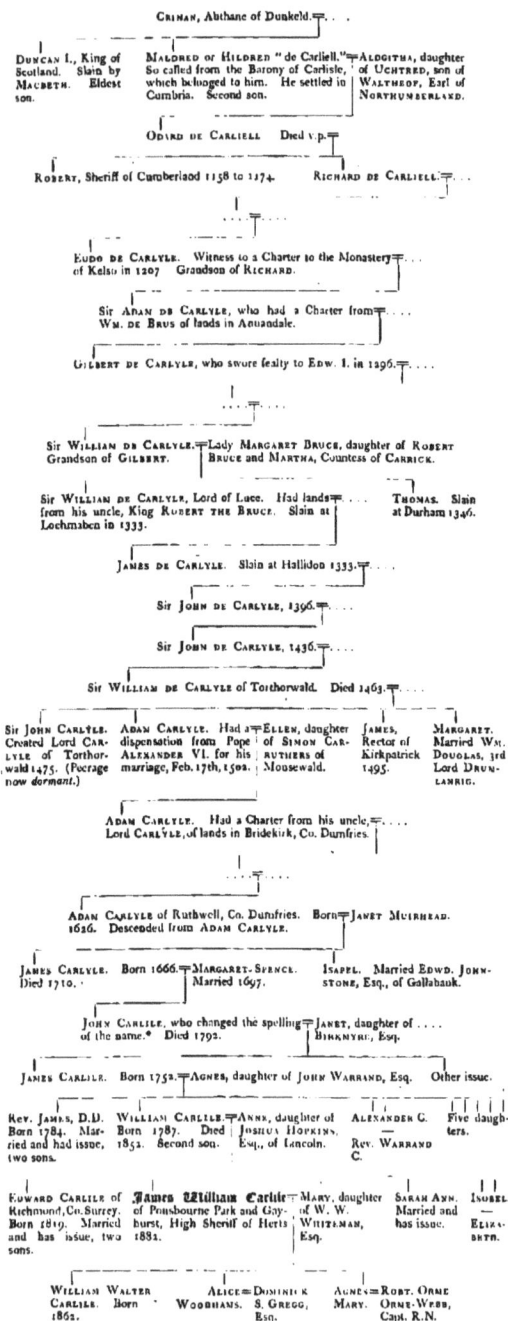

The Pedigree

OF THE

Family of Carlyle or Carlile,

DERIVED FROM

CRINAN, Abthane of Dunkeld. = . . .

DUNCAN I., King of Scotland. Slain by MACBETH. Eldest son.

MALDRED or HILDRED "de Carliell." So called from the Barony of Carlisle, which belonged to him. He settled in Cumbria. Second son. = ALDGITHA, daughter of UCHTRED, son of WALTHEOF, Earl of NORTHUMBERLAND.

ODARD DE CARLIELL Died v.p. =

ROBERT, Sheriff of Cumberland 1158 to 1174.

RICHARD DE CARLIELL. = . . .

. . . = . . .

EUDO DE CARLYLE. Witness to a Charter to the Monastery = . . . of Kelso in 1207 Grandson of RICHARD.

Sir ADAM DE CARLYLE, who had a Charter from = ... WM. DE BRUS of lands in Annandale.

GILBERT DE CARLYLE, who swore fealty to EDW. I. in 1296. = ...

. . . = ...

Sir WILLIAM DE CARLYLE. Grandson of GILBERT. = Lady MARGARET BRUCE, daughter of ROBERT BRUCE and MARTHA, Countess of CARRICK.

Sir WILLIAM DE CARLYLE, Lord of Luce. Had lands from his uncle, King ROBERT THE BRUCE. Slain at Lochmaben in 1333. = . . .

THOMAS. Slain at Durham 1346.

JAMES DE CARLYLE. Slain at Hallidon 1333. = ...

Sir JOHN DE CARLYLE, 1396. = . . .

Sir JOHN DE CARLYLE, 1436. = ...

Sir WILLIAM DE CARLYLE of Torthorwald. Died 1463. = ...

Sir JOHN CARLYLE. Created Lord CARLYLE of Torthorwald 1475. (Peerage now dormant.)

ADAM CARLYLE. Had a dispensation from Pope ALEXANDER VI. for his marriage, Feb. 17th, 1502. = ELLEN, daughter of SIMON CARRUTHERS of Moosewald.

JAMES, Rector of Kirkpatrick 1495.

MARGARET. Married WM. DOUGLAS, 3rd Lord DRUMLANRIG.

ADAM CARLYLE. Had a Charter from his uncle, = . . . Lord CARLYLE, of lands in Bridekirk, Co. Dumfries.

. . . = . . .

ADAM CARLYLE of Ruthwell, Co. Dumfries. Born 1626. Descended from ADAM CARLYLE. = JANET MUIRHEAD.

JAMES CARLYLE. Born 1666. Died 1710. = MARGARET SPENCE. Married 1697.

ISABEL. Married EDWD. JOHNSTONE, Esq., of Gallabank.

JOHN CARLILE, who changed the spelling of the name.* Died 1792. = JANET, daughter of . . . . BIRKMYRE, Esq.

JAMES CARLILE. Born 1752. = AGNES, daughter of JOHN WARRAND, Esq.

Other issue.

REV. JAMES, D.D. Born 1784. Married and had issue, two sons.

WILLIAM CARLILE. Born 1787. Died 1852. Second son. = ANNE, daughter of JOSHUA HOPKINS, Esq., of Lincoln.

ALEXANDER G. — REV. WARRAND C.

Five daughters.

EDWARD CARLILE of Richmond, Co. Surrey. Born 1819. Married and has issue, two sons.

JAMES WILLIAM CARLILE of Ponsbourne Park and Gayhurst, High Sheriff of Herts 1881. = MARY, daughter of W. W. WHITEMAN, Esq.

SARAH ANN. Married and has issue.

ISOBEL. — ELIZABETH.

WILLIAM WALTER CARLILE. Born 1862.

ALICE = DOMINICK WOODHAMS, S. GREGG, Esq.

AGNES = ROBT. ORME MARY. ORME-WEBB, Capt. R.N.

Hertfordshire.

❋❋❋❋❋❋

James William Carlile, Esq., of Ponsbourne Park, D.L. and a Magistrate for the County. High Sheriff 1882-3. Lord of the Manors of Temple Grafton, Co. Warwick, and Gayhurst with Stoke Goldington, Co. Bucks. Patron of two Livings. Late Major 6th West York Rifle Volunteers. Born 1823. Married, 1850, MARY, daughter of WALTER WOODHAMS WHITEMAN, Esq., of Glengarr, Co. Argyll, and has issue WILLIAM WALTER CARLILE, born 1862; ALICE WOODHAMS, married DOMINICK S. GREGG, Esq., of The Court, Temple Grafton, Co. Warwick; AGNES MARY, married Captain ROBERT ORME ORME-WEBB, R.N., second son of the Rev. R. HOLDEN WEBB, Rector of Essendon.

See Pedigree.

Arms.—Or, a cross flory gules, charged with a crescent of the first, on a chief of the second a saltire also of the first.

Crest.—Two dragon's heads, couped and addorsed vert.

Motto.—Humilitate.

Seats.—Ponsbourne Park, near Hertford; Gayhurst, near Newport Pagnell, Co. Bucks.

Club.—Junior Carlton.

Kent.

✸✸✸✸✸✸

Lieutenant-Colonel Henry Dorrien Streatfeild, J.P. and D.L. for the County of Kent. High Sheriff 1882–3. Lord of the Manor of Chiddingstone. Formerly Captain 1st Life Guards, late Lieutenant-Colonel Commanding West Kent Yeomanry Cavalry. Born 1825. Educated at Eton. Married, 1854, MARION HENRIETTA, youngest daughter of the late OSWALD SMITH of Blendon Hall, Co. Kent.

Arms.—Per fesse gules and sable, three bezants; quartering FREMLYN, TERRY, ASHDOWN, BEARD, and SIDNEY.

Crest.—An arm in armour proper, bent from the elbow, the fore-arm encircled with a band tied in knot gules; supporting a spear with a pennon, shewing argent, a St. George's cross, and gules, three bezants fessways on the sinister; the pennon being turned round the spear to shew part of both sides.

Motto.—Data fata secutus.

Seat.—Chiddingstone, Edenbridge, Kent.

Clubs.—White's and Carlton.

Pedigree.

ROBERT STREATFEILD of Chiddingstone,=. . . sister of Sir JOHN RIVERS, Co. Kent. Born 1514. Died 1559. Knt., Lord Mayor of London.

HENRY STREATFEILD of Chidding-=ALICE, daughter of HENRY stone. Died 1598. Moody, Esq., of London.

A

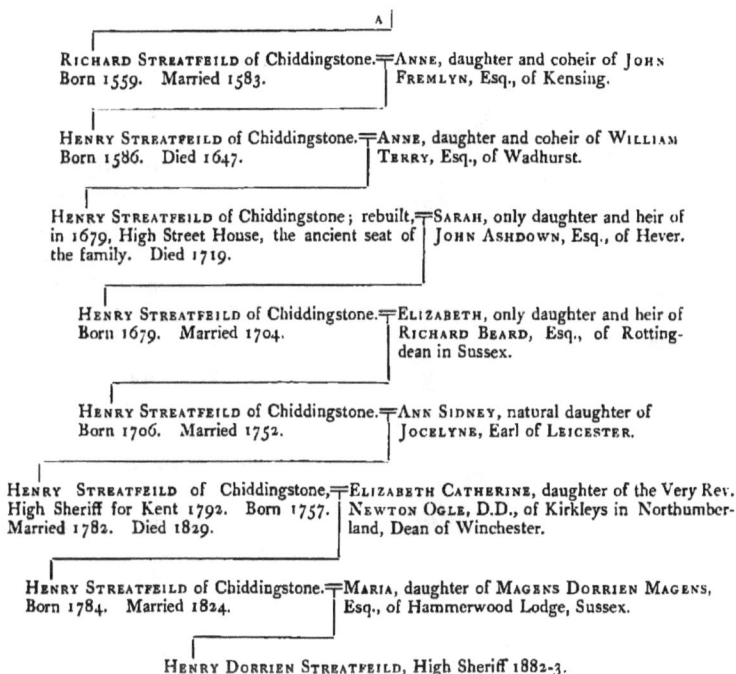

A

RICHARD STREATFEILD of Chiddingstone.⊤Anne, daughter and coheir of John
Born 1559. Married 1583. │ Fremlyn, Esq., of Kensing.

Henry Streatfeild of Chiddingstone.⊤Anne, daughter and coheir of William
Born 1586. Died 1647. │ Terry, Esq., of Wadhurst.

Henry Streatfeild of Chiddingstone; rebuilt,⊤Sarah, only daughter and heir of
in 1679, High Street House, the ancient seat of │ John Ashdown, Esq., of Hever.
the family. Died 1719.

Henry Streatfeild of Chiddingstone.⊤Elizabeth, only daughter and heir of
Born 1679. Married 1704. │ Richard Beard, Esq., of Rotting-
│ dean in Sussex.

Henry Streatfeild of Chiddingstone.⊤Ann Sidney, natural daughter of
Born 1706. Married 1752. │ Jocelyne, Earl of Leicester.

Henry Streatfeild of Chiddingstone,⊤Elizabeth Catherine, daughter of the Very Rev.
High Sheriff for Kent 1792. Born 1757. │ Newton Ogle, D.D., of Kirkleys in Northumber-
Married 1782. Died 1829. │ land, Dean of Winchester.

Henry Streatfeild of Chiddingstone.⊤Maria, daughter of Magens Dorrien Magens,
Born 1784. Married 1824. │ Esq., of Hammerwood Lodge, Sussex.

Henry Dorrien Streatfeild, High Sheriff 1882-3.

20

Lancashire.

❁❁❁❁❁

George McCorquodale, Esq.,

of The Willows, Newton-le-Willows, Lancashire, and Gadlys, Anglesey. A Magistrate and D.L. for Lancashire, and Hon. Colonel of the 19th Lancashire Rifle Volunteers. High Sheriff for Lancashire 1882-3. Born 1817. Married, first, Louisa Kate, daughter of Frederick Honan, Esq., of Cork, by whom he had issue; and, secondly, Emily, daughter of the Rev. Thomas Sanderson, D.D., Vicar of Great Doddington, Northamptonshire, by whom he also has issue.

Youngest son of

Hugh McCorquodale, Esq., of Liverpool, and Lucia, daughter of George Hall, Esq.

Arms.—Argent, a demi-stag gules, naissant out of a fesse tortille of the second and first.

Crest.—A stag standing at gaze proper.

Motto.—Vivat Rex.

Seats.—The Willows, Newton-le-Willows, Lancashire; and Gadlys, Anglesey.

Lincolnshire.

✥✥✥✥✥

Wm. Henry Smyth, Esq., of South Elkington, J.P. and D.L. for the County of Lincoln. High Sheriff 1882-3. High Steward of Louth, Lord of the Manor of South Elkington, and Patron of one Living. A Magistrate for the North Riding of Yorkshire. Born 1821. Educated at Harrow and Caius College, Cambridge. Married, 1849, SARAH ANNE, daughter of the late Rev. JOHN SARGEAUNT, and has, with other issue, WILLIAM GRENVILLE, born 1857.

Arms.—Per bend dancetté or and azure, a cross moline counterchanged; quartering WILLARBY, OTTEBY, LILBURNE, READING, and SHAN.

Crest.—Out of a ducal coronet or, a demi-falcon volant proper, wings expanded argent.

Seat.—Elkington Hall, South Elkington, Louth.

Pedigree.

JOHN SMITH, Esq., of Hacthorp, about the middle of the fourteenth century, married JANE, daughter and heir of ROBERT WILLARBY by ISABEL his wife, daughter and coheir of JOHN OTTEBY, son of Sir RANDOLPH DE OTTEBY. His direct descendant was—

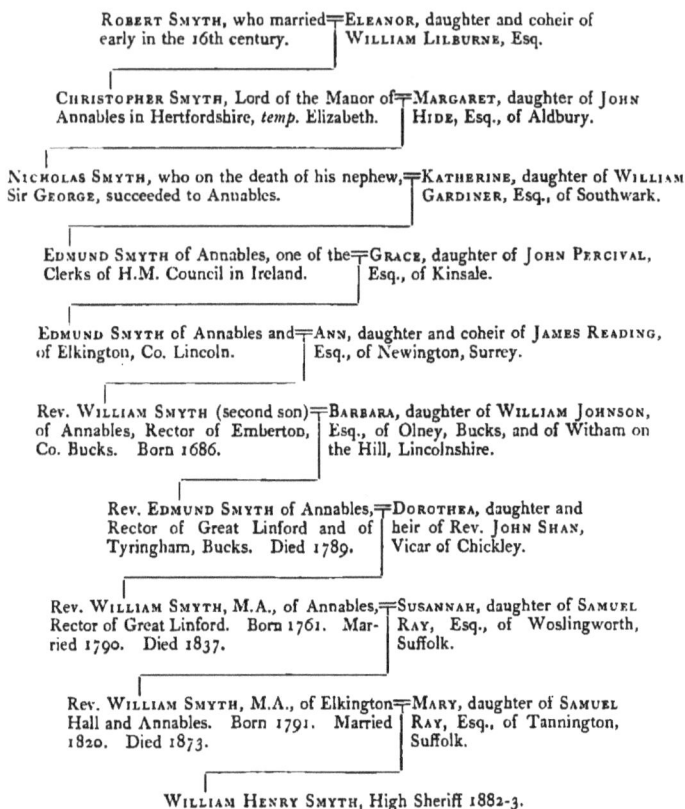

ROBERT SMYTH, who married⹋ELEANOR, daughter and coheir of
early in the 16th century. | WILLIAM LILBURNE, Esq.

CHRISTOPHER SMYTH, Lord of the Manor of⹋MARGARET, daughter of JOHN
Annables in Hertfordshire, *temp.* Elizabeth. | HIDE, Esq., of Aldbury.

NICHOLAS SMYTH, who on the death of his nephew,⹋KATHERINE, daughter of WILLIAM
Sir GEORGE, succeeded to Annables. | GARDINER, Esq., of Southwark.

EDMUND SMYTH of Annables, one of the⹋GRACE, daughter of JOHN PERCIVAL,
Clerks of H.M. Council in Ireland. | Esq., of Kinsale.

EDMUND SMYTH of Annables and⹋ANN, daughter and coheir of JAMES READING,
of Elkington, Co. Lincoln. | Esq., of Newington, Surrey.

Rev. WILLIAM SMYTH (second son)⹋BARBARA, daughter of WILLIAM JOHNSON,
of Annables, Rector of Emberton, | Esq., of Olney, Bucks, and of Witham on
Co. Bucks. Born 1686. | the Hill, Lincolnshire.

Rev. EDMUND SMYTH of Annables,⹋DOROTHEA, daughter and
Rector of Great Linford and of | heir of Rev. JOHN SHAN,
Tyringham, Bucks. Died 1789. | Vicar of Chickley.

Rev. WILLIAM SMYTH, M.A., of Annables,⹋SUSANNAH, daughter of SAMUEL
Rector of Great Linford. Born 1761. Mar- | RAY, Esq., of Woslingworth,
ried 1790. Died 1837. | Suffolk.

Rev. WILLIAM SMYTH, M.A., of Elkington⹋MARY, daughter of SAMUEL
Hall and Annables. Born 1791. Married | RAY, Esq., of Tannington,
1820. Died 1873. | Suffolk.

WILLIAM HENRY SMYTH, High Sheriff 1882-3.

Middlesex.

✥✥✥✥✥✥

Sir Reginald Hanson, Knt.

High Sheriff of the City of London and County of Middlesex 1881-2. Alderman of London, Commissioner of Lieutenancy of London, J.P. and D.L. of the Tower Hamlets, Hon. Colonel of 4th Battalion The Royal Fusiliers, Knight Commander of the "Couronne de Chêne" of the Netherlands, Member of the School Board for the City of London 1882. Born 31 May 1840. Educated at Rugby and Trinity College, Cambridge (M.A. 1868). Married, 10 May 1866, Constance Hallett, third daughter of Charles Bentley Bingley of Stanhope Park, Middlesex, Esq., and has issue two sons and two daughters.

Arms.—Or, a chevron counter-compony azure and argent, between three martlets sable.

Crest.—On a cap of maintenance azure, turned up argent, a martlet volant sable.

Motto.—Deo favente et sedulitate.

Residence.—4 Bryanston Square, W.

Clubs.—Oxford and Cambridge, Beaconsfield, and City Carlton.

For Pedigree, see next page.

Pedigree.

"Rogerus de Rastrick vixit temp. R. Henr. tertii (scilt. aº 1251) et tenuit terras in Rastrick, Clayton Bradforddale, prædium quoq' in Rastrick vocatum Linland et habuit servicium diversorum nativorum in eadem villa."—*Dugdale's Visitation of Yorkshire,* 1666.

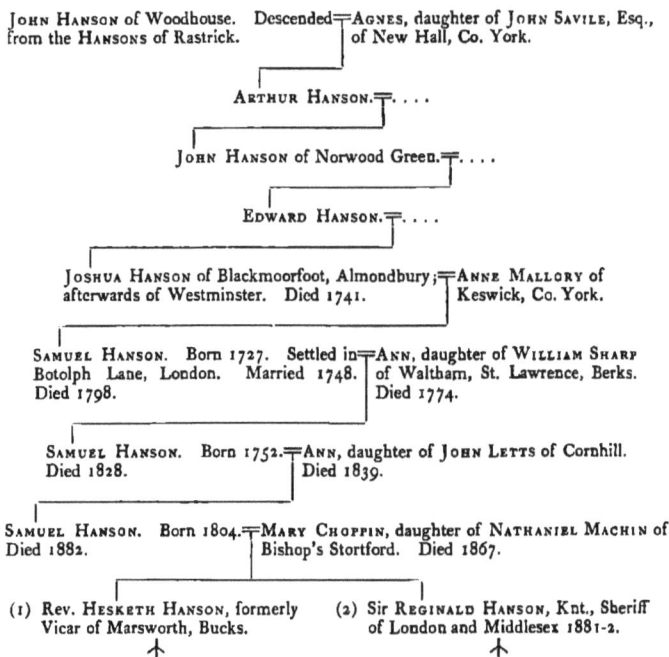

John Hanson of Woodhouse. Descended ⊤ Agnes, daughter of John Savile, Esq.,
from the Hansons of Rastrick. | of New Hall, Co. York.

Arthur Hanson. ⊤ ....

John Hanson of Norwood Green. ⊤ ....

Edward Hanson. ⊤ ....

Joshua Hanson of Blackmoorfoot, Almondbury; ⊤ Anne Mallory of
afterwards of Westminster. Died 1741. | Keswick, Co. York.

Samuel Hanson. Born 1727. Settled in ⊤ Ann, daughter of William Sharp
Botolph Lane, London. Married 1748. | of Waltham, St. Lawrence, Berks.
Died 1798. | Died 1774.

Samuel Hanson. Born 1752. ⊤ Ann, daughter of John Letts of Cornhill.
Died 1828. | Died 1839.

Samuel Hanson. Born 1804. ⊤ Mary Choppin, daughter of Nathaniel Machin of
Died 1882. | Bishop's Stortford. Died 1867.

(1) Rev. Hesketh Hanson, formerly   (2) Sir Reginald Hanson, Knt., Sheriff
Vicar of Marsworth, Bucks.   of London and Middlesex 1881-2.

Middlesex.

❊❊❊❊❊❊

Joseph Savory, Esq. High Sheriff for the City of London and County of Middlesex 1882–3. On the Livery of the Goldsmiths' and Poulters' Companies, a Director of the Royal Mail Steam Packet Company, Churchwarden of St. Mary Woolnoth, Lombard Street, Guardian of the Windsor Union, and holds several provincial appointments. Is senior partner in the Goldsmiths' Alliance Company, Limited, late A. B. Savory and Sons, of Cornhill, with which firm his family has been associated for nearly one hundred years. Born 1843. Educated at Harrow.

Eldest son of the late

Joseph Savory, Esq., of Buckhurst Park, Berks (who died 1879), and his wife Mary Caroline, daughter of J. Braithwaite, Esq., of Kendal, Westmoreland, and Scotby, Cumberland.

Lineage.

Mr. Savory is a direct descendant of a Huguenot family belonging to the old French nobility, who took refuge in this country on the Revocation of the Edict of Nantes.

Arms.—Paly of six argent and vert, a chief sable.
Crest.—A cubit arm erect, holding a cap of maintenance, between two branches of laurel in orle. **Motto.**—Vincit omnia veritas.
Seat.—Buckhurst Park, Sunninghill, Berkshire. **Club.**—National.

(See also Sheriffs of Cities, etc.)

Note.—The Sheriffs of the County of Middlesex and City of London are appointed by the Citizens of London, who had the privilege of appointment granted to them by King Henry I. This right was afterwards confirmed by King John.

E

26

Monmouthshire.

✿✿✿✿✿✿

Thomas Phillips Price, Esq., of Triley Court, a Magistrate for the County of Monmouth. High Sheriff 1882-3. Lord of the Manor and Patron of Kemeys Commander, Co. Monmouth. Captain Royal Monmouthshire Engineer Militia, and a Barrister-at-Law. Born 1844. Educated at Winchester and University College, Oxford (B.A. 1867, M.A. 1868). Married, 17th January 1882, FRANCES ANN, daughter of the Rev. T. C. ROWLATT.

Only son of the late

Rev. William Price, Vicar of Llanarth, Co. Monmouth, and Canon of Llandaff, who died 1878. Married MARY, daughter of the late THOMAS PHILLIPS, Esq., of Llanellen, Co. Monmouth, and sister of the late Sir THOMAS PHILLIPS, Q.C.

Arms.—Quarterly—1 and 4. Argent, three boar's heads couped sable. 2 and 3. Per bend sinister, ermine and ermines, a lion rampant or. (The arms of ELYSTAN GLODRYDD, Founder of the Fourth Royal Tribe, from whom this family of PRICE is lineally descended.)

Crest.—A lion rampant reguardant or.

Motto.—Gwell angau neu chibillpdd.

Seat.—Triley Court, Abergavenny.

Clubs.—The Union and The Devonshire.

Norfolk.

✦✦✦✦✦✦

Sir Henry George Paston-Bedingfeld, Bart., J.P. and D.L. for the County of Norfolk. High Sheriff 1882–3. Lord of the Manors of Oxburgh and Bedingfeld, and Patron of one Living. Formerly in the Austrian Cuirassiers, and late Captain West Norfolk Militia. Born 1830. Educated at Stonyhurst College. Succeeded as 7th Bart. 1862.

Married, 1859, AUGUSTA LUCY, only child of EDWARD JOHN CLAVERING, Esq., of Callaly Castle, Northumberland, by whom he has issue a son and heir, HENRY EDWARD, born 1860.

Descended from OGERUS DE PUGES, a Norman, who after the Conquest obtained the Manor of Bedingfeld in Suffolk.

The Manor of Oxburgh came into the family by the marriage of Sir EDMUND BEDINGFELD (who died 1446) with MARGARET, sister and coh. of ROBERT DE TUDDENHAM. (*See Pedigree.*)

Arms.—Ermine, an eagle displayed gules; quartering PASTON, and on an escutcheon of pretence CLAVERING of Callaly Castle.

Crest.—A demi-eagle, wings expanded, gules.

Motto.—*Despicio terrena solem contemplor.*

Badge.—A fetterlock (the badge of the House of York), granted by Edward IV.

Seat.—Oxburgh, near Stoke Ferry, Norfolk.

Residence.—45 Cromwell Houses, South Kensington.

Club.—Reform.

For Pedigree, see next page.

Pedigree.

Sir EDMUND BEDINGFELD, Knt., became Lord of Oxbury by his marriage with MARGARET, sister and coheir of ROBERT DE TUDDENHAM. His great-great-grandson, Sir HENRY BEDINGFELD, Knt., was one of the first who declared for Queen Mary, and for his services was made Knight Marshal of Her Majesty's Army, Captain of the Guards, Governor of the Tower of London, and a Privy Councillor. He married CATHERINE, daughter of Sir ROGER TOWNSHEND, a Judge of the Court of Common Pleas. His great-grandson, Sir HENRY BEDINGFELD, Knt., a zealous Royalist, was made prisoner during the Civil Wars, and committed to the Tower, dying soon after his release. He married, first, ELIZABETH, daughter of Lord WILLIAM HOWARD; secondly, ELIZABETH, daughter and coheir of PETER HOUGHTON, Esq., of Houghton Tower, Co. Lancaster, and was succeeded by his only surviving son—

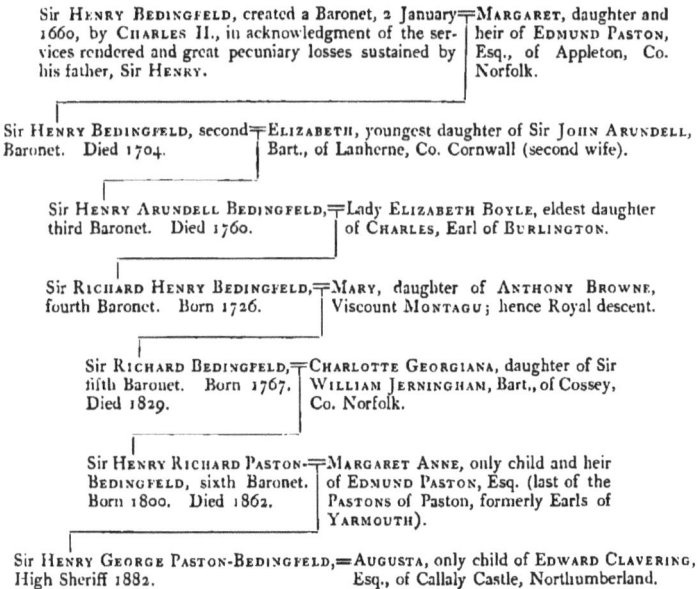

Sir HENRY BEDINGFELD, created a Baronet, 2 January═MARGARET, daughter and 1660, by CHARLES II., in acknowledgment of the ser-│heir of EDMUND PASTON, vices rendered and great pecuniary losses sustained by│Esq., of Appleton, Co. his father, Sir HENRY.│Norfolk.

Sir HENRY BEDINGFELD, second═ELIZABETH, youngest daughter of Sir JOHN ARUNDELL, Baronet. Died 1704.│Bart., of Lanherne, Co. Cornwall (second wife).

Sir HENRY ARUNDELL BEDINGFELD,═Lady ELIZABETH BOYLE, eldest daughter third Baronet. Died 1760.│of CHARLES, Earl of BURLINGTON.

Sir RICHARD HENRY BEDINGFELD,═MARY, daughter of ANTHONY BROWNE, fourth Baronet. Born 1726.│Viscount MONTAGU; hence Royal descent.

Sir RICHARD BEDINGFELD,═CHARLOTTE GEORGIANA, daughter of Sir fifth Baronet. Born 1767.│WILLIAM JERNINGHAM, Bart., of Cossey, Died 1829.│Co. Norfolk.

Sir HENRY RICHARD PASTON-═MARGARET ANNE, only child and heir BEDINGFELD, sixth Baronet.│of EDMUND PASTON, Esq. (last of the Born 1800. Died 1862.│PASTONS of Paston, formerly Earls of │YARMOUTH).

Sir HENRY GEORGE PASTON-BEDINGFELD,═AUGUSTA, only child of EDWARD CLAVERING, High Sheriff 1882.│Esq., of Callaly Castle, Northumberland.

Northamptonshire.

✠✠✠✠✠✠

Richard Henry Ainsworth, Esq., a Magistrate for the County of Lancaster. High Sheriff for Northamptonshire 1882–3. Lord of the Manor of Halliwell. Patron of one Living. Major Duke of Lancaster's Own Yeomanry. Born 1839. Educated at Eton and Christ Church, Oxford. Married, 1866, ISABELLA MARGARET, daughter of JOHN JAMES VAUGHAN, Rector of Gotham, Notts. Succeeded his uncle 1870.

Descent.

This family has been resident in the township of Halliwell for two hundred years.

PETER AINSWORTH of The Moss.⹜

PETER AINSWORTH of Light-⹜ALICE ASPINALL of Carrington, bounds, Co. Lancaster. | Co. Chester. Married 1761.

RICHARD AINSWORTH of ⹜SARAH, daughter of JAMES NOBLE, Moss Bank, Halliwell. | Esq., of Lancaster.

PETER AINSWORTH of Smithills, eldest son and heir, J.P., D.L., and M.P. Died s.p. 1870, succeeded by his nephew.

JOHN HORROCKS⹜ELIZABETH, daughter of JOHN AINSWORTH of | SHAW, Esq., of London. Moss Bank. | Married 1833.

RICHARD HENRY AINSWORTH, High Sheriff 1882–3.

Arms.—Gules, three battle-axes argent.

Crest.—A man in armour, holding a battle-axe proper.

Motto.—Mea gloria fides.

Seats.—Smithills Hall and Moss Bank, Bolton, Lancashire; Winwick Warren, Rugby.

Clubs.—Oxford and Cambridge and The New University.

CRESSA NE CAREAT

𝔑orthumberland.

✪✪✪✪✪

𝔒swin Cumming Baker=Cresswell, Esq., of Cresswell, a Magistrate for Northumberland. High Sheriff 1882-3. Patron of one Living. Major Northumberland Militia, formerly Captain 3rd Hussars. Born 1844. Educated at Eton and Christ Church, Oxford (B.A. 1866, M.A. 1875). Married, 1872, EMMA SOPHIA GEORGIANA, daughter of the Hon. RICHARD DENMAN of Westergate, Sussex, and has, with other issue, ADDISON FRANCIS, born 1874.

Arms.—Quarterly—1 and 4. Erminois, three torteaux, two and one, each charged with a squirrel sejant argent. [CRESSWELL.] 2 and 3. Gules, a goat statant argent, armed and crined or, between three saltiers of the last. [BAKER.]

Crests.—1. On a mount vert a torteau charged with a squirrel sejant argent. [CRESSWELL.] 2. A goat's head erased argent, armed and crined or, gorged with a collar gemel, and charged on the neck with a saltier gules. [BAKER.]

Motto.—Cressa ne careat.

Seats.—Cresswell, near Morpeth ; Harehope Hall, Alnwick, Northumberland.

Residence.—3 Hereford Gardens, W.

Club.—Army and Navy.

For Pedigree, see next page.

Pedigree.

This ancient family has been seated in the North of England from a very early period, ROBERT DE CRESSWELL, who lived in the time of King Richard I., being then in possession of the estate.

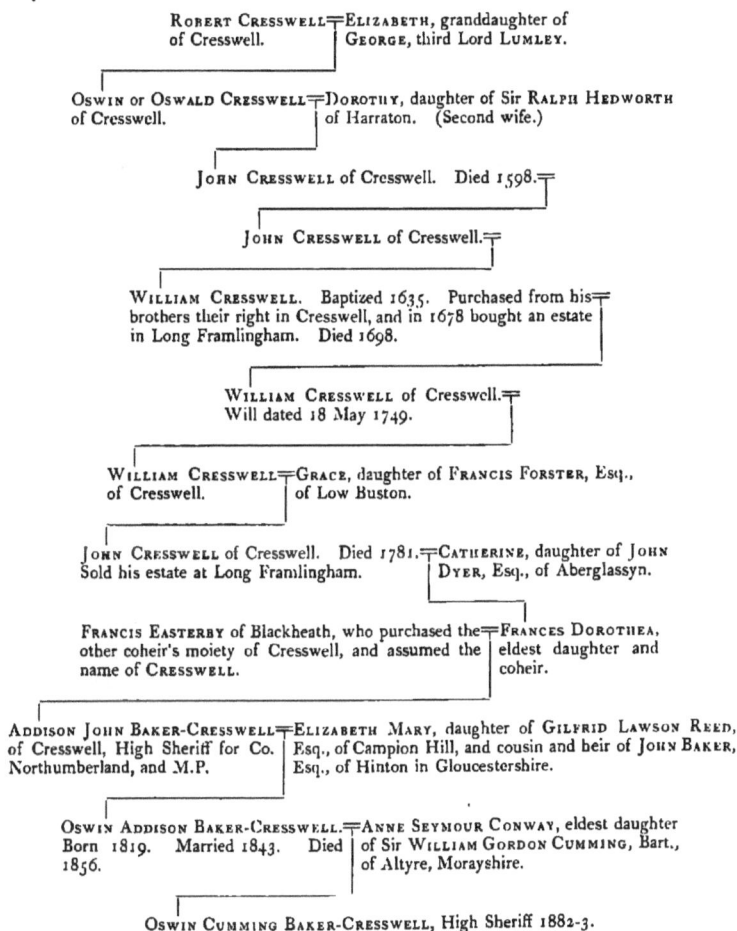

ROBERT CRESSWELL╤ELIZABETH, granddaughter of
of Cresswell. │ GEORGE, third Lord LUMLEY.

OSWIN or OSWALD CRESSWELL╤DOROTHY, daughter of Sir RALPH HEDWORTH
of Cresswell. │ of Harraton. (Second wife.)

JOHN CRESSWELL of Cresswell. Died 1598.╤

JOHN CRESSWELL of Cresswell.╤

WILLIAM CRESSWELL. Baptized 1635. Purchased from his╤
brothers their right in Cresswell, and in 1678 bought an estate │
in Long Framlingham. Died 1698.

WILLIAM CRESSWELL of Cresswell.╤
Will dated 18 May 1749. │

WILLIAM CRESSWELL╤GRACE, daughter of FRANCIS FORSTER, Esq.,
of Cresswell. │ of Low Buston.

JOHN CRESSWELL of Cresswell. Died 1781.╤CATHERINE, daughter of JOHN
Sold his estate at Long Framlingham. │ DYER, Esq., of Aberglassyn.

FRANCIS EASTERBY of Blackheath, who purchased the╤FRANCES DOROTHEA,
other coheir's moiety of Cresswell, and assumed the │ eldest daughter and
name of CRESSWELL. │ coheir.

ADDISON JOHN BAKER-CRESSWELL╤ELIZABETH MARY, daughter of GILFRID LAWSON REED,
of Cresswell, High Sheriff for Co. │ Esq., of Campion Hill, and cousin and heir of JOHN BAKER,
Northumberland, and M.P. │ Esq., of Hinton in Gloucestershire.

OSWIN ADDISON BAKER-CRESSWELL.╤ANNE SEYMOUR CONWAY, eldest daughter
Born 1819. Married 1843. Died │ of Sir WILLIAM GORDON CUMMING, Bart.,
1856. │ of Altyre, Morayshire.

OSWIN CUMMING BAKER-CRESSWELL, High Sheriff 1882-3.

Nottinghamshire.

✪✪✪✪✪✪

Sir Henry Bromley, Bart., J.P. and D.L.   High Sheriff 1882–3.
Late Captain 3rd Notts Rifle Volunteers, formerly Captain 48th
Regiment.   Born 1816.   Married first, 1848, CHARLOTTE FRANCES ANNE,
daughter of Col. LANCELOT ROLLESTON, M.P., by whom he had issue;
secondly, 1856, GEORGIANA ELLEN, daughter of VERE FANE, Esq., of Little
Ponton Hall, Co. Lincoln.

Arms.—Quarterly per fesse indented gules and or.
Crest.—A cock-pheasant sitting proper.
Motto.—Pensez fort.
Seat.—Stoke Hall, Newark.

Oxfordshire.

✪✪✪✪✪✪

Edward Slater Harrison, Esq., J.P.   High Sheriff 1882–3.
Captain Oxfordshire Yeomanry, late Captain Oxfordshire Militia.
Lord of the Manors of Newton Purcell, with Shelswell, Fringford, Hethe, and
Mixbury.   Born 1832.   Married, 1865, CECELIA, daughter of Col. SAUNDER-
SON of Northbrook House, Hunts.

This family of HARRISON has been settled for some time in the County of Oxford.

Rutland.

❦❦❦❦❦❦

John William Handley Davenport-Handley, Esq.,

D.L. for Rutland, and a Magistrate for the County of Chester. High Sheriff for Rutland 1882-3. Lord of the Manor and Patron of Clipsham. Born 19 Oct. 1851. Educated at Harrow and Magdalene College, Cambridge. Married, 1876, FANNY CONSTANCE MABEL, youngest daughter of the late JOHN JERVIS BROADWOOD, Esq., of Buchan Hill, Sussex, and has issue JOHN, born 1878, and CHARLES, born 1879.

Assumed the additional surname and arms of HANDLEY on the death of his uncle, JOHN HANDLEY, Esq., of Clipsham.

Arms.—Quarterly—1 and 4. Argent, in fesse between two cottises three mascles gules, between as many goats passant sable, armed or. [HANDLEY.] 2 and 3. Argent, a chevron between three crosses-crosslet fitché sable, a canton azure. [DAVENPORT.]

Crests.—1. A goat passant sable, armed or, holding in the mouth a trefoil slipped, and charged on the body with two mascles interlaced or. 2. A man's head couped at the shoulders in profile, a rope round the neck, and charged on the breast with a cross-crosslet fitché sable.

Mottoes.—Audaces fortuna juvat. Perseverando.

Seat.—Clipsham Hall, near Oakham.

Club.—The Windham.

For Pedigree, see next page.

Pedigree.

On the paternal side Mr. DAVENPORT-HANDLEY descends from the Welsh family of HUMPHREYS, whose progenitor was EDWIN AP GRONO, Lord of Teigaingl in Flintshire, and Founder of the Twelfth Noble Tribe of Wales. Twenty-fourth in descent from this Chieftain was the Rev. EVAN HUMPHREYS.

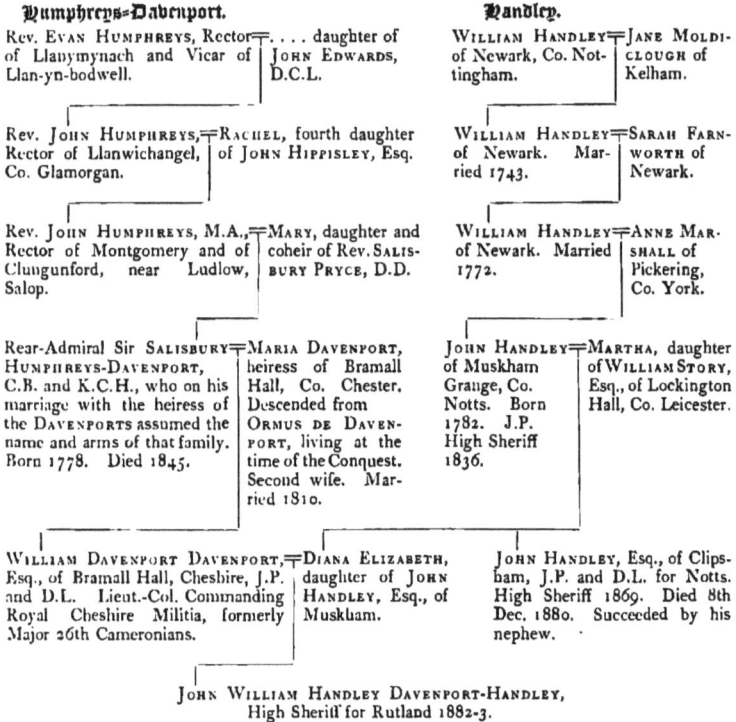

Humphreys-Davenport.

Rev. EVAN HUMPHREYS, Rector ⹋ .... daughter of
of Llanymynach and Vicar of | JOHN EDWARDS,
Llan-yn-bodwell. | D.C.L.

Rev. JOHN HUMPHREYS, ⹋ RACHEL, fourth daughter
Rector of Llanwichangel, | of JOHN HIPPISLEY, Esq.
Co. Glamorgan.

Rev. JOHN HUMPHREYS, M.A., ⹋ MARY, daughter and
Rector of Montgomery and of | coheir of Rev. SALIS-
Clungunford, near Ludlow, | BURY PRYCE, D.D.
Salop.

Rear-Admiral Sir SALISBURY ⹋ MARIA DAVENPORT,
HUMPHREYS-DAVENPORT, | heiress of Bramall
C.B. and K.C.H., who on his | Hall, Co. Chester.
marriage with the heiress of | Descended from
the DAVENPORTS assumed the | ORMUS DE DAVEN-
name and arms of that family. | PORT, living at the
Born 1778. Died 1845. | time of the Conquest.
| Second wife. Mar-
| ried 1810.

WILLIAM DAVENPORT DAVENPORT, ⹋ DIANA ELIZABETH,
Esq., of Bramall Hall, Cheshire, J.P. | daughter of JOHN
and D.L. Lieut.-Col. Commanding | HANDLEY, Esq., of
Royal Cheshire Militia, formerly | Muskham.
Major 26th Cameronians.

Handley.

WILLIAM HANDLEY ⹋ JANE MOLDI-
of Newark, Co. Not- | CLOUGH of
tingham. | Kelham.

WILLIAM HANDLEY ⹋ SARAH FARN-
of Newark. Mar- | WORTH of
ried 1743. | Newark.

WILLIAM HANDLEY ⹋ ANNE MAR-
of Newark. Married | SHALL of
1772. | Pickering,
| Co. York.

JOHN HANDLEY ⹋ MARTHA, daughter
of Muskham | of WILLIAM STORY,
Grange, Co. | Esq., of Lockington
Notts. Born | Hall, Co. Leicester.
1782. J.P. |
High Sheriff |
1836. |

JOHN HANDLEY, Esq., of Clipsham, J.P. and D.L. for Notts.
High Sheriff 1869. Died 8th
Dec. 1880. Succeeded by his
nephew.

JOHN WILLIAM HANDLEY DAVENPORT-HANDLEY,
High Sheriff for Rutland 1882-3.

Shropshire.

✦✦✦✦✦✦

James Jenkinson Bibby, Esq., of Hardwicke Grange, a Magistrate and Deputy Lieutenant for the County. High Sheriff 1882–3. Born 1813. Married, 1844, SARAH, daughter of THOMAS COOK, Esq., of Dewsbury in the County of York.

Younger son of

John Bibby, Esq., of Liverpool, who married MARY, daughter of JOSEPH MILLARD of Newcastle under Lyne.

———— 1299841

Arms.—Azure, on a saltier argent, between two escallops in pale or, and as many mullets in fesse of the second, a lion rampant gules.

Crest.—A dexter arm erect, holding in the hand a dagger in bend sinister, all proper.

Motto.—Fi et virtute.

Seat.—Hardwicke Grange, near Shrewsbury.

Clubs.—Junior Carlton and Conservative.

BROADMEAD.

THOMAS · PALFREY · ENMORE · PARK

SEMPER FIDELIS

Somersetshire.

❋❋❋❋❋

**Thomas Palfrey Broad=
mead, Esq.**, of Enmore
Park, Justice of the Peace and
Deputy Lieutenant for the County.
High Sheriff 1882-3. A Barrister-
at-Law. Born 29 April 1822.
Educated at Trinity College, Cam-
bridge. Called to the Bar at Inner
Temple 1847. Married, 16 Aug.
1848, HARRIET, only child of
JAMES BUCKNELL, Esq., of Cork
and Crowcombe, Somersetshire, and
has, with other issue, JAMES BUCK-
NELL, born 1849; educated at Harrow and Trinity College, Cambridge;
married ANGELINA ISABELLA, younger daughter of the late HENRY JAMES
HOARE, Esq., of Morden Lodge, Surrey.

Son of the late

Philip Broadmead, Esq., of Olands, J.P. and D.L. Born 1789. Married ELIZA-
BETH, only child of THOMAS PALFREY, Esq., of Oake and Milverton, Somersetshire.

This family was residing at the end of the sixteenth century in the neighbourhood
of Silverton, Devon, where it remained till about the year 1750, when PHILIP, eldest son
of GILBERT BROADMEAD, settled at Milverton in the County of Somerset.

Arms.—Argent, in base on a mount a stag lodged proper, and on a chief azure
three acorns slipped or. On an escutcheon of pretence, for BUCKNELL,
Argent, two chevrons gules between three buck's heads cabossed sable.

Crest.—On a wreath of the colours a fret azure, thereon a stag's head erased,
holding in the mouth an acorn, slipped proper.

Motto.—Semper fidelis.

Seats.—Enmore Park, Bridgwater, and Olands, Milverton, Somersetshire.

Staffordshire.

✠✠✠✠✠

John Robinson, Esq., of Westwood Hall, a Magistrate and Deputy Lieutenant for the County of Stafford. High Sheriff 1882-3. Born 1823. Married, 1848, HELEN, daughter of the late JOHN LEES, Esq., of Newton Solney, Co. Derby, and has, with other issue, Rev. ARTHUR EDWARD, born 1851, educated at Repton School and Trinity College, Cambridge.

Eldest son of the late

John Robinson, Esq., of Ravenshaw, Skipton, Co. York.

Arms.—Vert, a chevron between three stags trippant or.

Crest.—A stag, as in the arms.

Motto.—Virtute non verbis.

Seats.—Westwood Hall, Leek (purchased in 1868 from the Davenports), and Brown How, Blawith, near Ulverstone.

Club.—The National, Whitehall Gardens.

Suffolk.

✠✠✠✠✠

Edward Philippe Mackenzie, Esq., of Auchenskeoch and Downham Hall. High Sheriff for Suffolk 1882-3. A Magistrate for Cos. Suffolk, Norfolk, and Dumfries. Captain Suffolk Yeomanry, formerly Lieutenant 9th Lancers. Late Chairman Thetford Board of Guardians. Born 1842. Educated at Harrow and St. John's College, Oxford. Married, 1865, ELLEN JANE, third daughter of HENRY

BASKERVILLE, Esq., D.L., of Crowsley Park, Oxfordshire, and has issue
BERYL MARIE BASKERVILLE.

Pedigree.

Descended from the MACKENZIES of Fairburn, Co. Ross.

ALEXANDER MACKENZIE. Born 1765, at Fairburn.⸗MARY, daughter
Educated at Inverness High School.   Afterwards in   of WILLIAM
partnership with DAVID MACKINTOSH, celebrated as | ROBERTS, Esq.
Canal Engineers.   Died at Blackburn, Co. Lancaster. | Died 1828.

| WILLIAM MACKENZIE of Newbie and Auchenskeoch. Partner in the eminent firm of MACKENZIE and BRASSEY. A Director of Railways. Chevalier of the Legion of Honour. Claimant to the Muirton Estate. Succeeded by his brother EDWARD. | EDWARD MACKENZIE of Fawley Court, Bucks.   J.P. for Cos. Buckingham, Oxford, Dumfries, and Kirkcudbright. D.L. Oxford and High Sheriff 1862. Born 1 May 1811.   Purchased the Mansion and Estates of Fawley Court 1853. Seventh son. | ⸗MARY, daughter of WILLIAM DALZIEL, Esq., of The Craigs, Co. Dumfries. |

EDWARD PHILIPPE MACKENZIE, Esq.   High⸗HELEN JANE
Sheriff of Suffolk 1882-3.   Second son. | BASKERVILLE.

BERYL MARIE BASKERVILLE.

Arms.—Or, a cross parted and fretty azure, between in the first and fourth quarters a stag's head cabossed of the last, in the second and third quarters a mountain in flames proper.

Crest.—A stag's head cabossed azure, within its attires a cross couped or, the whole between two stag's attires gold.

Motto.—Always faithful.

Seats.—Downham Hall, Brandon, Suffolk ; Auchenskeoch, Southwick, Stewartry of Kirkcudbright ; The Craigs, Dumfriesshire.

Residence.—19 Wimpole Street, W.

Club.—Junior Carlton.

HENRY·JOHN·TRITTON

Fortiter gerit crucem.

Surrey.

✠✠✠✠✠✠

Henry John Tritton, Esq.,

D.L. and a Magistrate for the County of Surrey. High Sheriff 1882-3. Lord of the Manor of Tadworth, and Major Middlesex Yeomanry Cavalry, formerly Captain King's Own Militia. Born 1842. Educated at Eton. Married, 1866, ANNA, daughter of RICHARD BULLER, Esq., of Lanreath, Co. Cornwall, and has issue HENRY MAXWELL.

Eldest son of the late

Henry Tritton, Esq., of Beddington, Surrey, by his wife ELIZABETH, daughter of CHARLES MAXWELL, Esq.

Arms.—Argent, on a bend gules an esquire's helmet or.

Crest.—A horse passant argent.

Motto.—*Fortiter gerit crucem.*

Seat.—Tadworth Court, Epsom.

DONALD LARNACH ESQ

SANS PEUR

BRAMBLETYE EAST GRINSTEAD

Sussex.

✦✦✦✦✦✦

Donald Larnach, Esq., Lord of the Manor of Brambletye. High Sheriff for the County of Sussex 1882-3. Formerly a Merchant and Banker of Australia. Born 1817. Married, 1845, JANE ELIZABETH, daughter of WILLIAM WALKER, Esq., of Sydney, New South Wales.

Fifth son of the late

William Larnach, Esq., of Caithness, N.B., who died in 1829.

Arms.—Gules, a boar's head erased close, between three mullets in chief and three crosses-crosslet fitché in base, all within a bordure argent.

Crest.—A cat salient.

Motto.—Sans peur.

Seat.—Brambletye, East Grinstead, Sussex.

Club.—City of London, Broad Street.

Warwickshire.

✠✠✠✠✠✠

Lieut.-Colonel Charles William Paulet, a Magistrate for Co.
Warwick.   High Sheriff 1882-3.   Lieut.-Colonel Warwickshire
Yeomanry, formerly 7th Hussars.   Born 1832.   Married, 1863, SUSAN
AMELIA GEORGINA, daughter of the late WILLIAM STANDISH STANDISH,
Esq., and has issue.

For Descent, see Marquis of WINCHESTER.

Arms.—Sable, three swords in pile, points in base argent, hilts and pommels or.

Crest.—A falcon, wings displayed or, belled of the same, and gorged with a ducal
coronet gules.

Motto.—Aymez loyaulté.

Seat.—Wellesbourne House, Warwick.

Club.—Army and Navy.

G

Westmorland.

✠✠✠✠✠✠

William Thompson, Esq., of Moresdale Hall, Deputy Lieutenant and Magistrate for the County. High Sheriff 1882-3. Born 1836. Educated at Blackheath, Kent. Married JESSIE, only daughter of W. B. WATKINS, Esq., of Llandaff, Co. Glamorgan, and has issue WATKINS WILLIAM, born 18 Aug. 1882.

Third son of

James Thompson, Esq., of Moresdale, by BETSY, daughter of HENRY RAUTHMELL, Esq., Bridge End, Old Hutton, Westmorland.

The THOMPSONS of Gragrigg Head (the ancient estate) have been owners of landed property in the County of Westmorland for many generations.

Arms.—Azure, a lion passant guardant or within a bordure argent.

Crest.—A lion rampant or.

Motto.—Spectemur agendo.

Seat.—Moresdale Hall, near Kendal.

𝔚iltshire.

✠✠✠✠✠✠

𝔗he Right Honourable Edward Pleydell-Bouverie, of East
Lavington, a Magistrate for Berkshire and Wiltshire. High Sheriff for
the latter County 1882–3. Was Under-Secretary for the Home Department
1850–2. Vice-President of the Board of Trade and Chairman of Committees
1853–5. President of Poor Law Board 1855–8. M.P. for Kilmarnock
1844–74. Born 26 April 1818. Married, November 1842, ELIZABETH
ANNE, youngest daughter of the late General BALFOUR of Balbirnie, and has
issue WALTER, born 1848.

Second son of

William, third Earl of RADNOR.

Descended from LAURENCE DES BOUVERIES, a native of Flanders, born 1542, who
came to England and settled at Canterbury.

Arms.—1 and 4. Per fesse or and argent, an eagle displayed with two heads sable,
on the breast an escutcheon gules charged with a bend vair. [BOUVERIE.]
2 and 3. Argent, a bend gules gutté d'eau between two ravens sable, a
chief chequy or and of the last. [PLEYDELL.]

Crest.—A demi-eagle reguardant, wings elevated sable, gorged with a ducal coronet
or, charged on the breast with a cross-crosslet argent.

Motto.—Patria cara, carior libertas.

Seat.—East Lavington Manor, Devizes.

Club.—Brooks'.

𝕎orcestershire.

✠✠✠✠✠✠

George Edward Martin, Esq., J.P. and D.L. for the County.
High Sheriff 1882-3. Captain Queen's Own Worcestershire Yeomanry
Cavalry. Lord of the Manor of Upton on Severn. Born 11 Nov. 1829.
Educated at Eton and Merton College, Oxford. Married, 15 Oct. 1862,
Maria Henrietta, daughter of the late Benjamin Cherry, Esq., of
Brickendon Grange, Co. Hertford, J.P. and D.L., and has, with other issue,
Eliot George Bromley.

Lineage.

Mr. Martin of Ham Court descends from William Martin of Evesham,
Co. Worcester, Gentleman, born 1583, Mayor of the Borough and J.P., who married,
June 1610, Anne, daughter of Philip Yardner of Evesham, Gentleman.

Arms.—Quarterly—1 and 4. Paly of six erminois and azure, on a chief engrailed
gules three martlets argent. [Martin.] 2 and 3. Argent, on a chevron
sable between three falcon's heads erased gules as many cinquefoils or.
[Jackson.]

Crest.—On a wreath of the colours a mount vert, thereon a martin proper, resting
the dexter forepaw on a bezant.

Motto.—Pejus letho flagitium.

Seat.—Ham Court, near Worcester.

Clubs.—Arthur's and The Athenæum.

‬orkshire.

✱✱✱✱✱✱

Sir Henry Day Ingilby,
Bart., J.P. and D.L. for the
West Riding. High Sheriff for York-
shire 1882–3. A Magistrate for the
County of Berwick. Lord of the
Manors of Ripley, Dacre, and North
Deighton, and Patron of two Livings.
Born 1826. Educated at Magdalen
College, Oxford; B.A. 1848, M.A.
1851. Married, 1862, the Hon. ALICIA
MARGARET, youngest daughter and
coheir of the Right Hon. DAVID
ROBERTSON, Baron MARJORIBANKS (extinct).

Descent.

This ancient Family was originally of Engelbi, near Lincoln, and the name was
spelt in that way until settling at Ripley, and in an inscription in the Old Tower at
Ripley, 1555, it is INGLBI.

The first of the Family of whom we have record was Sir THOMAS DE INGLEBY,
Knt., one of the Justices of Common Pleas and King's Bench 30 Sept. 1361, Judge of
Assize 1351, and Knight of the Shire 1349. Married EDELINE, daughter of . . . .
RIPLEY of Ripley Castle. Buried at Ripley.

Eleventh in descent was WILLIAM INGILBY, a volunteer at Marston Moor, created
a Baronet by King Charles I., 17 May 1642. This Baronetcy became extinct in 1772.
Revived in 1781 in favour of JOHN INGILBY, Esq., of Ripley, and extinct in 1854.
Again revived, 1866, in favour of the Rev. HENRY JOHN INGILBY, M.A. (the father of
the present Baronet), who was born 1790; married, 1824, ELIZABETH, second daughter
of DAY HART MACDOWALL, Esq., of Walkinshaw, N.B.; and died 4 July 1870.

For Arms, etc., see next page.

Ancient Arms.—Sable, a star of six rays argent.

Arms.—Sable, an estoile argent within a bordure engrailed gobony or and gules, and on an escutcheon of pretence (for ROBERTSON, Baron MARJORIBANKS) Gules, three wolves' heads erased argent, armed and langued azure.

Crest.—A boar's head couped and erect argent, tusked or, in the mouth an estoile of the last.

Motto.—Mon Droit.

Seats.—Ripley Castle, Yorks ; Harrington Hall, Spilsby, Lincolnshire.

Residence.—9 Hereford Gardens, Park Lane.

Clubs.—Boodle's and Oxford and Cambridge.

North Wales.

Anglesey.

✣✣✣✣✣✣

Hugh Edwards, Esq., of Tynrideen, J.P. and D.L. for the County. High Sheriff 1882-3. Born 1832. Educated partly in England and Wales. Married, 1863, to MARGARET ANN, second daughter of the late Captain WILLIAM OWEN, Towyn Lodge.

Fourth son of the late

Thomas Edwards, Esq., of Pwllpillo, by MARGARET, youngest daughter of the late JOHN HUGHES, Esq., of Tynrideen, Anglesey.

Seat.—Rose Mount, Holyhead, Anglesey.

Carnarvonshire.

✦✦✦✦✦✦

Joseph Evans, Esq.,

J.P. for Cos. Lancashire and Denbighshire, and Lord of the Manor of Parr, Co. Lancashire. High Sheriff for the County 1882–3. Of Hurst House, near Prescot, and Haydock Grange, Co. Lancashire ; Macnau House, Co. Carnarvon ; and Llanddogget Park, Co. Denbighshire. Born 4 Sept. 1817.

Second son of the late

Richard Evans, Esq., of Haydock Grange, Co. Lancashire, who died 1864.

A branch of the EVANS Family, descended from BROCHWEL YSGITHROG, Prince of Powis, 617—"EVANS of Hafodwen (Marrington)"—which settled in the neighbourhoo of Montgomery, Churchstoke, and Chirbury, Co. Montgomery, N.W.

Arms.—Sable, three nag's heads erased argent, on a chief nebuly or, a pale gules charged with an estoile of the third between two estoiles of the fourth.

Crest.—On a wreath of the colours a nag's head erased argent between two estoiles or.

Motto.—A fynno Duw derfid.

Seat.—Hurst House, Prescot, Lancashire.

Club.—Devonshire.

Denbighshire.

❋❋❋❋❋❋

John Fairfax Jesse, Esq., J.P. and D.L. for the County of Denbigh. High Sheriff 1882–3. Born 1851. Succeeded his brother 1865.

Only surviving son of the late

John Jesse, Esq., J.P., F.R.S., of Llanbedr, High Sheriff in 1856.

Arms.—Argent, three dog-fish.

Crest.—A demi-lion rampant.

Seat.—Caerfron, Llanbedr, Ruthin.

Flintshire.

❋❋❋❋❋❋

Sir William Grenville Williams, Bart., J.P. and D.L. for the County Flint. High Sheriff 1882–3. A Magistrate for Co. Denbigh. Formerly of the Royal Dragoons, and late Captain 1st Life Guards. Born 1844. Educated at Eton. Succeeded his father 1876.

Arms.—Argent, two foxes countersaliant in saltire gules, a crescent for difference.

Crest.—An eagle displayed or.

Motto.—Cadarn ar cyfrwys.

Seats.—Bodelwyddan, Pengwern, Rhyl, Flintshire; Bodidris, Llandegla, Denbighshire.

Clubs.—Carlton and Naval and Military.

H

50

Merionethshire.

✦✦✦✦✦✦

Charles Reynolds Williams,

Esq., of Dolmelynllyn. High Sheriff 1882-3. Born at Baroche, in the Presidency of Bombay. Married, 1846, MARGARET, only daughter of JOHN ROMER, Esq., Member of the Council of Bombay, and subsequently Acting Governor of that Presidency. Has issue ROMER and two daughters.

Is the son of

Colonel Monier Williams, Surveyor-General of Bombay, whose brother, Colonel GEORGE WILLIAMS, at the age of twelve, in company with his uncle, Major GRIFFITHS WILLIAMS, R.A., joined the Army in North America under General BURGOYNE, and carried the flag of truce to the enemy's camp on the surrender at Saratoga. He was afterwards M.P. for Ashton under Lyne. Colonel MONIER WILLIAMS married HANNAH SOPHIA, daughter of THOMAS BROWN, Esq., E.I.C.S.

Arms.—Gules, a chevron ermine between three Saxon's heads couped proper.

Crest.—A stag's head.

Motto.—Si je puis.

Seat.—Dolmelynllyn, Dolgelly, an ancient residence formerly belonging to the VAUGHANS, situated in the romantic vale of the Maw.

Club.—The Union, Trafalgar Square.

Montgomeryshire.

✦✦✦✦✦✦

Nicholas Watson Fairles-Humphreys, Esq., a Magistrate for the County of Montgomery. High Sheriff 1882-3. Born 1834. Married, 1876, MICAELA DE LAS MERCEDES, only daughter and heiress of RICHARD SMITH HUMPHREYS, Esq., J.P., of Bank House, Montgomery.

Son of

William Watson Fairles, Esq., of Field House, South Shields.

The Family of FAIRLES derive their name from lands belonging to them A.D. 1360 in Wolsingham, County of Durham. Allied to several other old and distinguished families of the North of England—BULMERS, CONYERS, NEWTONS, BURDONS, OTWAYS, etc.

Arms.—Or, a lion rampant gules, holding between the paws a star of the last, debruised by a bendlet azure; and on an escutcheon of pretence, for HUMPHREYS—Sable, three nag's heads couped argent.

Crest.—An unicorn's head, couped argent, horned or.

Motto.—I am ready.

Seat.—Bank House, Montgomery.

South Wales.

James Lewis, Esq., of Plâs-draw, Glamorganshire, and Pwll-Ivor, Breconshire. J.P. for both Counties. On the Roll for Sheriffs for 1878, and served the office of High Sheriff for the County of Brecon 1882–3. Born 1826. Educated at Cowbridge. Married, 1867, Louisa Catherine, youngest daughter of the Rev. William Edwards, Vicar of Llangollen, Denbighshire, and has, with other issue, a son, James Windsor, born in 1877.

Arms.—Gules, three chevronels in pale argent; being the Arms borne by Jestyn ap Gwrgan.

Crest.—A Paschal lamb proper.

Motto.—Duw fo; O fy rhan.

Seat.—Plâs-draw, Aberdare, Glamorganshire.

Club.—Hanover Square.

For Pedigree, see next page.

Pedigree.

Mr. JAMES LEWIS is of a junior branch of one of the ancient families of the Principality, being descended in a direct line from MADOC, second son of JESTYN AP GWRGAN, who was a tributary Prince of Glamorgan, and Founder of the Fifth Royal Tribe of Powys. Fourth in descent from MADOC was Sir DAVID, parson of St. Fagan's, who married CATHERINE, daughter and sole heiress of JEVAN GOCH of Rhydlavar, by whom he acquired that estate, which remained in the family until JOAN, the only child of LEWIS AP LLEWELYN AP LEWIS AP LLEWELYN, of Rhydlavar, married WILLIAM, son of JOHN THOMAS of Llanbradach. Their descendants held it for several generations, and still quarter the Arms. From the last-named LLEWELYN of Rhydlavar the descent is thus continued:—

Cadet Branch.

Morgan ap Llewelyn, second son.=.... daughter of
Settled at Michaelstone Court, St. Fagan's. | THOMAS BACH.

LEWIS LLEWELYN.=.... daughter of WILLIAM LEWIS AP PHILIP.

EDWARD **Lewis** of The Court, the first=.... daughter of THOMAS PRICHARD,
who assumed the surname. | Registrar of Llandaff.

HENRY LEWIS=MARY EDWARDS of Maes-y-Chrochan, by a daughter
of The Court. | of LAMBROOK STRADLING of St. Donats.

WILLIAM LEWIS of The Court.=REBECCA SPARROW of Llwyn-yr-eos.

EDWARD LEWIS of The Court.=CATHERINE THOMAS of Park-Coed, Marchan.

EDWARD LEWIS of the Great House,=ELIZABETH, daughter of JAMES EVANS, Esq.,
second son. | of Fairwater.

EDWARD LEWIS, second son.=ELIZABETH, daughter of EVAN DAVID of Fairwater.

James Lewis of Plàs-draw, third son.=LOUISA CATHERINE, daughter of
High Sheriff 1882-3. | Rev. WILLIAM EDWARDS.

JAMES WINDSOR LEWIS.

Cardiganshire.

❈❈❈❈❈❈

Charles Lloyd, Esq., a Magistrate for the County, and High Sheriff
1882–3. Born at Bettws Bledrws Rectory 20 May 1850. Educated at
Marlborough College, Wilts, and Oriel College, Oxford (B.A. 1872, M.A.
1879). Married, 1876, MARGARET MACFIE, daughter of DUNCAN ALEX-
ANDER CAMPBELL, Esq., and has issue ALISTER CAMPBELL BOWEN, born 1878.

The LLOYDS of Waunifor trace their descent from CADIFOR AP DINAWAL, Lord
of Castell Howel, and GILFACHWEN (seventh in descent from RODERICK the Great),
who, when the Normans were harassing Wales, won renown by taking, by escalade, the
Castle of Cardigan from the Earl of CLARE and the Flemings, 1155. The arms given
him for this exploit are now borne by his descendants.

>   **Arms.**—Sable, a spear-head imbrued, between three scaling ladders argent, on a
>   chief gules a castle triple-towered of the second.
>   **Crest.**—A lion rampant argent.
>   **Motto.**—Sic itur ad astra.
>   **Seat.**—Waunifor, Maesycrugiau, Carmarthenshire.

Carmarthenshire.

❈❈❈❈❈❈

Thomas Morris, Esq., of Coombe, a Magistrate for the County.
High Sheriff 1882–3. Born 1849. Married, 1857, MARY, daughter
of JAMES LLOYD, Esq., and has issue.

Glamorganshire.

✿✿✿✿✿✿

Sir Joseph Layton Elmes Spearman, Bart., a Magistrate for the County of Glamorgan. High Sheriff 1882-3. Captain Royal Glamorgan Artillery Militia. Born 1857. Educated at Eton and Brasenose College, Oxford. Succeeded his grandfather 1874. Married, 1878, ETHEL, eldest daughter of WILLIAM LEASK, Esq., and has issue two sons—JOSEPH WILLIAM, born 1879, and ALEXANDER YOUNG, born 1881.

———————

The progenitor of Sir JOSEPH's family was a cadet of the SPEARMANS of Dunnington, Co. Salop, seated there since the Conquest, and supposed to be descended from the old Lords of Aspromonte.

Arms.—Azure, on a chevron ermine between three tilting-spears argent, headed or, a red-deer's head erased proper; quartering ATKINSON, PATTISON, WHITFIELD, and BROMLEY.

Crest.—A lion rampant proper, gorged with a collar gemell or, supporting a tilting-spear, also proper, enfiled with a mural crown gold.

Motto.—Dum spiro spero.

Residence.—Llanelay Hall, Llantrisant.

Seats.—Llansannor Court, Cowbridge, Glamorganshire; and The Spring, Hanwell.

Clubs.—New University and Junior Carlton.

Pembrokeshire.

❋❋❋❋❋

Charles Edward Gregg Philipps, Esq., of Picton Castle, Lord Lieutenant and Custos Rotulorum of Haverfordwest, J.P. for Carmarthenshire and Pembrokeshire. High Sheriff of Pembrokeshire 1882-3. Captain Pembroke Yeomanry Cavalry. Born 6 October 1840. Educated at Cheltenham College. Called to the Bar at the Middle Temple June 1868. Married, 25 June 1868, MARY PHILIPPA, daughter and coheir of the Rev. JAMES HENRY ALEXANDER PHILIPPS of Picton Castle, and has, with other issue, HENRY ERASMUS EDWARD.

Mr. PHILIPPS (who, in compliance with a testamentary injunction of his father-in-law, by Royal Licence, dated 29 July 1876, assumed the surname and quartered the arms of PHILIPPS) is the

Eldest son of

Edward Fisher, Esq., of Springdale, Co. York.

(*See Pedigree, next page.*)

Arms.—Quarterly—1 and 4. Argent, a lion rampant sable, gorged with a ducal coronet, and therefrom a chain reflexed over the back or, and for distinction a cross-crosslet. [PHILIPPS.] 2 and 3. Argent, on a chevron gules three trefoils slipped of the field, in chief as many fleurs-de-lis of the second. [FISHER.]

Crests.—1. A lion rampant, as in the arms. [PHILIPPS.] 2. In front of a bulrush erect a kingfisher proper, resting dexter claw on a fleur-de-lis or.

Mottoes.—Ducit amor patriæ.
  Virtute et fide.

Seat.—Picton Castle, Haverfordwest.

Residence.—7 Kensington Palace Gardens, W.

Clubs.—Carlton, Junior Carlton, and The Salisbury.

𝔓𝔢𝔡𝔦𝔤𝔯𝔢𝔢 𝔬𝔣 𝔓𝔥𝔦𝔩𝔦𝔭𝔭𝔰 𝔬𝔣 𝔓𝔦𝔠𝔱𝔬𝔫 ℭ𝔞𝔰𝔱𝔩𝔢.

This family is one of the most ancient in Wales, being descended from CADIFOR AP COLHOYN, Lord of Dyfed in Pembrokeshire, otherwise called CADIFOR VAWR, or The Great, of Blaen Kich, Lord of Kilsant. He died A.D. 1034. Tenth in descent was Sir THOMAS, with whom this pedigree commences.

Sir THOMAS AP PHILIP.=JANE, daughter of Sir HENRY DONNE, Knt., of Picton, who inherited
Knighted *circa* 1511. that estate in right of his mother, CATHERINE, daughter and coheir of
Acquired Picton Castle Sir JOHN WOGAN of Picton, whose ancestor, Sir JOHN WOGAN of
by marriage. Wiston, had acquired Picton by his marriage with JOAN, daughter and
heir of Sir WILLIAM PICTON of Picton, Knt.

JOHN PHILIPS of Picton.=ELIZABETH, daughter of Sir WILLIAM GRIFFITH of Penrhyn,
Died 1551. Co. Carnarvon, Chamberlain of North Wales.

MORGAN. Succeeded to Picton Castle=ELIZABETH, daughter of RICHARD
on death of his brother WILLIAM. FLETCHER of Bangor.

Sir JOHN PHILIPS of Picton. Created=ANN, daughter of Sir JOHN PERROTT of
a Baronet 1621. Died 1629. Haroldston, Knt., Lord Deputy of Ireland.

Sir RICHARD PHILIPS, 2nd Bart.=ELIZABETH, daughter of Sir ERASMUS DRYDEN, Bart.

Sir ERASMUS PHILIPPS, 3rd Bart., who changed=CATHERINE, daughter and coheir of
the spelling of the name. Died 1697. EDWARD DARCY, Esq. Second wife.

Sir JOHN PHILIPPS. Died 1736.=MARY, daughter and heir of ANTHONY SMITH, Esq., of Surat.

BULKELEY PHILIPPS of Aber-=PHILIPPA, daughter of WILLIAM
cover, Co. Carmarthen, ADAMS of Pembroke, Esq.
youngest son. Died 1776.

𝔉𝔦𝔰𝔥𝔢𝔯.

EDWARD FISHER,=ELIZABETH, | JAMES CHILD, Esq., of=MARIA PHILIPPA ARTEMESIA,
Esq., of Thorn, daughter of | Bigilly House, Co. Pem- only daughter and heir. Died
Co. York. .... BRADY, | broke. Died 1815. 1786.
Esq.

JOHN FISHER, Esq.,=PHŒBE, only daughter | Rev. HENRY GWYTHER,=MARIA ARTEMESIA,
of Spring Dale. Born of J. SHARPLES, Esq., | M.A., Vicar of Yardley, only daughter and
1767. Married of Hitchin, Herts. | Co. Worcester. Died heir. Married 1812.
1800. Died 1840. | 1872. Second husband. Died 1852.
A | B

I

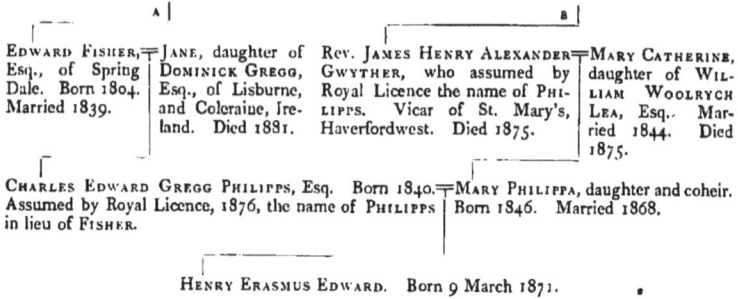

58

EDWARD FISHER,⊤JANE, daughter of
Esq., of Spring | DOMINICK GREGG,
Dale. Born 1804. | Esq., of Lisburne,
Married 1839. | and Coleraine, Ire-
| land. Died 1881.

Rev. JAMES HENRY ALEXANDER⊤MARY CATHERINE,
GWYTHER, who assumed by | daughter of WIL-
Royal Licence the name of PHI- | LIAM WOOLRYCH
LIPPS. Vicar of St. Mary's, | LEA, Esq., Mar-
Haverfordwest. Died 1875. | ried 1844. Died
| 1875.

CHARLES EDWARD GREGG PHILIPPS, Esq. Born 1840.⊤MARY PHILIPPA, daughter and coheir.
Assumed by Royal Licence, 1876, the name of PHILIPPS | Born 1846. Married 1868.
in lieu of FISHER.

HENRY ERASMUS EDWARD. Born 9 March 1871.

𝕽 adnorshire.

✪✪✪✪✪

Charles Coltman Rogers, Esq., J.P., D.L., and High Sheriff

1882-3 for Radnorshire. A Magistrate for Cos. Hereford and Salop.
Lord of the Manor of Stanage, and Patron of one Living. Born May 1854.
Educated at Eton and Brasenose College, Oxford (B.A. 1876, M.A. 1879).

The direct ancestor of Mr. ROGERS was ROGER DE NORBURY of Lydbury, North
Salop. His great-grandson, ROGER DE NORBURY, married MARGERY, daughter of
THOMAS SCHIRE DE LA HOME, and became possessed of estates in Home 1314. Their
son, JOHN ROGERS DE LA HOME, took the surname of ROGERS from his father's
Christian name, and by deed, dated Thursday after the Feast of the Holy Trinity, 36
Edward III., obtained from PHILIP DE MERCER all his estate in Home, which has since
remained in the family.

Arms.—Argent, on a chevron vert between three bucks courant sable five ermine
spots gold.

Crest.—A buck's head sable, charged with three ermine spots or, erased gules,
attired of the second.

Motto.—Celeriter et jucunde.

Seat.—Stanage Park, Brampton Bryan, Herefordshire.

Club.—Brooks' and New University.

Sheriffs of Cities, Towns, and Counties

THEREOF

WHO BEAR COAT ARMOUR,

AND SUBSCRIBERS, WHOSE NAMES ARE MARKED THUS (*).

———◆———

1881—2.

Bristol .	. *WILLIAM EDWARDS GEORGE, Downside, Stoke Bishop, near Bristol.	
Gloucester .	. *JOSEPH KARN .	. Page 61
Hull .	. *HENRY BRIGGS	„ 62
London	. Sir W. A. OGG	„ 63
	(*See also County of Middlesex.*)	
Norwich	. *JAMES JOHN WINTER	„ 63
Poole .	. *JAMES POWELL GODWIN, Perry Gardens, Poole.	
York	. *WALTER CATTLEY . .	„ 64

1882—3.

Bristol .	. *JOHN LYSAGHT .	. Page 65
London .	. *POLYDORE DE KEYSER . . .	„ 67
	(*See also County of Middlesex.*)	
Newcastle on Tyne	. *HENRY CLAPHAM .	„ 68
York .	. *JOSEPH SYKES RYMER .	„ 69

1881—2.

City and County of Gloucester.

✠✠✠✠✠

Joseph Karn, Esq., of Villa Vinaria, Hillfield, Gloucester. High Sheriff for the City and County of Gloucester 1881–2. Born 12 Sept. 1815. Married, 9 May 1847, ELIZA, daughter of THOMAS WHERRETT, Esq., of Cheltenham.

Arms.—Ermine, on a bend sable five annulets or.
Crest.—Out of a heart a hand issuing, holding a scimitar proper.
Motto.—Esse quam videre.

Town and County of Hull.

✦✦✦✦✦✦

Henry Briggs, Esq., J.P., of Elmfield Cottingham, Magistrate for the Borough of Hull, and Sheriff of the Town and County of Kingston upon Hull 1881-2. Born 1816. Married, 1843, MARIA, eldest daughter of B. UNTHANK, Esq., of Stockton on Tees.

Arms.—Argent, a bend vair between three escutcheons sable, each charged with a pheon of the field, a bordure engrailed bezantée.

Crest.—A mount vert, thereon, in front of a lion passant ermine, the dexter paw resting upon a pheon sable, a laurel branch erect proper.

Motto.—Fortiter et fideliter.

Seat.—Elmfield Cottingham.

City of London and County of Middlesex.

✠✠✠✠✠✠

Sir William Anderson Ogg, Sheriff of London and Middlesex 1881-2. Knighted for his services in connection with the opening, by Her Majesty, of Epping Forest, 1882.

Arms.—Azure, a saltire engrailed or, between in fesse two stag's heads erased, and in pale by as many castles.

Crest.—A dexter and a sinister arm, habited, in the hands proper a thistle erect, and between the arms a wreath of laurel.

Motto.—*Fugiendo vincimus.*

Residence.—Hampton House, Brentwood.

City and County of Norwich.

✠✠✠✠✠✠

James John Winter, Esq., of Higham House, Norwich. Sheriff of the City and County of Norwich 1881-2. Married Sophia Catherine, eldest daughter of the Rev. Charles Barnwell Barnwell, of Mileham Hall, Norfolk, and Sophia his wife (before her marriage Wyndham of Cromer Hall, Norfolk), and has issue four daughters—Sophia Wyndham, Adelaide Maud Marion, Mabel Grace, and Arabella Catherine. His only son, Wyndham Barnwell Winter, died in 1871.

Eldest son of

James Winter, Esq., of Drayton Lodge, Norfolk.

Arms.—Chequy or and azure, a fesse argent.

Crest.—A hind passant argent, ducally gorged, lined and ringed or.

Motto.—*Semper non frigidus.*

City and County of York.

❊❊❊❊❊❊

Walter Cattley, Esq., of Ashfield, York. Sheriff for the County of the City of York 1881–2. Born 12 Aug. 1834. Educated at the Royal School of Saint Peter, York. Married, Oct. 1859, LUCY JUDITH, third daughter of the Rev. THOMAS PYM WILLIAMSON, Vicar of Fenny Stratford, Bucks, and has issue one son and eight daughters.

Fifth and youngest son of

John Henry Cattley of York (whose brother, THOMAS CATTLEY, was Sheriff of York 1816), by FRANCES DOROTHY, eldest daughter of THOMAS CATTLEY of Clapham, Surrey, formerly H.E.I.C.S.

Descended from an ancient Lincolnshire Family. The direct ancestor of the above-named WALTER CATTLEY was settled near York some years prior to, and was present at, the Battle of Marston Moor, and thenceforth the Family have resided uninterruptedly in York and its vicinity to the present time, as prominent merchants.

Arms.—Quarterly—1 and 4. Gules, on a chevron engrailed between three anchors or, two lions rampant guardant respecting azure. 2. Gules, six escallops argent, 3, 2, and 1. 3. Argent, three bars and in chief as many lozenges azure, on a canton or, a fess of the second.

Crest.—A demi-cat (or according to some authorities a demi-leopard) proper rampant guardant, supporting an anchor with cable or.

Motto.—Caute non astute.

Seat.—Ashfield, near York.

Club.—The St. Leonard's, York.

1882—3.

City and County of Bristol.

⊛⊛⊛⊛⊛

John Lysaght, Esq., Sheriff for the City and County of Bristol 1882-3. Married ELLEN, daughter of Lieutenant SIDNEY Moss, R.N.

Arms.—Argent, three spears erect gules, on a chief azure a lion passant guardant or.

Crest.—A dexter arm embowed in armour, the hand holding a sword, all proper.

Motto.—Bella, horrida bella. The ancient Motto was **Lamb laidir an nachtar**—i.e "The strongest hand uppermost."

Residence.—Springfort, Stoke Bishop, Bristol.

Pedigree.

The LYSAGHTS, originally "O'BRIAN," are of an ancient family in Ireland, and about the time of BRIAN BORU were first called GILUSACHT, which means "Sons of the powerful." The tradition is that they were so called after the Battle of Clontarf, when

K

Brian Boru defeated the Danes. The name was afterwards spelt in various ways, as appears in original deeds. In records of the time of Edward II. and III. it is Leyssagh. In a map of Ireland, about 1600, is the name of Mac Gillysaght as the owner of a large tract of land in the north-west of Co. Clare; and in Inquisitions taken about 1629 and 1630 it is M'Lysagh, McLyshagh, and M'Lissagh.

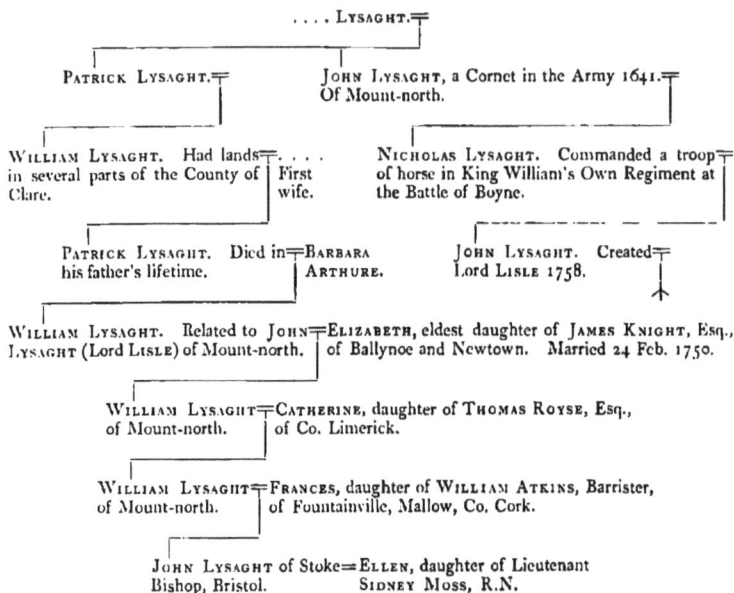

.... Lysaght.⊤

Patrick Lysaght.⊤   John Lysaght, a Cornet in the Army 1641.⊤
                          Of Mount-north.

William Lysaght. Had lands⊤. . . .   Nicholas Lysaght. Commanded a troop⊤
in several parts of the County of | First   of horse in King William's Own Regiment at
Clare. | wife.   the Battle of Boyne.

Patrick Lysaght. Died in⊤Barbara   John Lysaght. Created⊤
his father's lifetime. | Arthure. Lord Lisle 1758.

William Lysaght. Related to John⊤Elizabeth, eldest daughter of James Knight, Esq.,
Lysaght (Lord Lisle) of Mount-north. | of Ballynoe and Newtown. Married 24 Feb. 1750.

William Lysaght⊤Catherine, daughter of Thomas Royse, Esq.,
of Mount-north. | of Co. Limerick.

William Lysaght⊤Frances, daughter of William Atkins, Barrister,
of Mount-north. | of Fountainville, Mallow, Co. Cork.

John Lysaght of Stoke=Ellen, daughter of Lieutenant
Bishop, Bristol.   Sidney Moss, R.N.

City of London and County of Middlesex.

⊕⊕⊕⊕⊕⊕

Polydore de Keyser, Esq., F.S.A. and F.R.G.S., Alderman of the Ward of Farringdon Without. Sheriff of the City of London and County of Middlesex 1882-3. For fifteen years a Member of the Court of Common Council. A Governor of Bridewell, Bethlehem Hospital, and St. Bartholomew's Hospital, and a Freeman of the Spectacle-makers' Company. Formerly Chairman of the Bridge House Estate Committee and of the Guildhall School of Music. Born 13 Dec. 1832, at Termonde in Belgium. Privately educated in England, Brussels, and Germany. Married, 1862, LOUISE, eldest daughter of the late M. J. PIERON of Brussels.

Son of the late

M. C. de Keyser, Founder of the Royal Hotel, Blackfriars (who in 1856 returned to Brussels, where he died 1862), and ROSALIE TROCH, daughter of Dr. CHARLES TROCH of Termonde.

———————

Arms.—Azure, a saltire chequy or and gules, on a chief of the second a fasces between two mallets.

Crest.—A mallet between two branches of palm in orle.

Motto.—Respice aspice prospice.

Residence.—Chatham House, Grove Road, Clapham Park.

Club.—City Liberal.

City and County of Newcastle on Tyne.

✪✪✪✪✪✪

Henry Clapham, Esq., Justice of the Peace. Sheriff of the City and County of Newcastle on Tyne 1882-3. Steam Ship Owner. Born at Benwell Grove, Newcastle on Tyne, 25 February 1827.

Son of

Anthony Clapham, Esq., of Newcastle on Tyne, Chemical Manufacturer.

Arms.—Argent, on a bend azure six fleurs-de-lis or, two, two, and two.

Crest.—A lion rampant sable, holding in his dexter paw a sword argent, hilt and pommel or.

Residence.—Jesmond Cottage, Newcastle on Tyne.

City and County of York.

✦✦✦✦✦✦

Joseph Sykes Rymer, Esq.

High Sheriff for the City and County of York 1882–3. For fifteen years a Member of the York Corporation, of which body his father and grandfather were also Members. Born in the City of York 27 February 1841. Married, 1 March 1864, SARAH, youngest daughter of the late JOHN LEETHAM, Esq., Shipowner, of York.

The family of RYMER is of considerable antiquity, and the name is upon the Roll of the Norman Knights who came over with William the Conqueror, found in Battle Abbey at the dissolution of the Monasteries. (See Fuller's 'Church History of Great Britain.')

Shaw, in his 'General Chronology of England' (page 103), says, " And now because those Houses may not be unremembered unto whom King William disposed the lands and possessions of this Realm for their good service, I have thought good to publish the names of them as heretofore I have done out of the Chronicles of Normandy gathered by William Tayleur of Rhoan—' The Archers of the Vale of Rueill and of Brehicill and of many other places.' The second name is ' Le Sire de la Rimer.' "

Arms.—Vaire argent and gules within a bordure azure bezanté.

Crest.—A hand holding a sword erect proper.

Motto.—Ense animus major.

Residence.—13 Park Place, York.

www.ingramcontent.com/pod-product-compliance
Lightning Source LLC
Chambersburg PA
CBHW021524270326
41930CB00008B/1078